THE SPIRITUAL MENTOR

OTHER BOOKS BY
DR. JAMES GRASSI

THE SPIRITUAL MENTOR

JIM **GRASSI**

THOMAS NELSON
Since 1798

NASHVILLE   DALLAS   MEXICO CITY   RIO DE JANEIRO

Published in Nashville, Tennessee, by Thomas Nelson. Thomas Nelson is a registered trademark of HarperCollins Christian Publishing, Inc.

Page design and layout: Crosslin Creative
Images: VectorStock

Thomas Nelson titles may be purchased in bulk for educational, business, fund-raising, or sales promotional use. For information, please e-mail SpecialMarkets@ ThomasNelson.com.

Unless otherwise noted, Scripture quotations are taken from the New King James Version. © 1982 by Thomas Nelson. Used by permission. All rights reserved.

Scripture quotations marked The Voice are taken from The Voice™ translation. © 2012 Ecclesia Bible Society. Used by permission. All rights reserved.

ISBN: 978-1-4016-7791-6

Printed in the United States of America

13 14 15 16 17 18 RRD 6 5 4 3 2 1

Dedicated to my faithful wife and best friend,
Louise Grassi, a Proverbs 31 Woman, and to all the faithful
men's ministry leaders who help make men's ministry happen

Imitate me, just as I also imitate Christ. Now I praise you, brethren, that you remember me in all things and keep the traditions just as I delivered them to you. But I want you to know that the head of every man is Christ, the head of woman is man, and the head of Christ is God.

1 Corinthians 11:1–3

Let all of us be imitators of our Lord!

CONTENTS

FOREWORD

Are you tired of hearing people talk about mentoring and discipleship while not seeing it truly lived out in their lives? If you're like me, you find yourself wishing someone would simply step up and lead the charge to live out this calling Christ has given to us.

The book you hold in your hands is just such a clarion call. And it has come at the exact right time too. I believe there has never been a time when spiritual mentors have been needed more desperately.

Over the past two thousand years, Jesus' plan for reaching and transforming the lives of people hasn't changed. The principles of discipleship and spiritual mentorship are as powerful today as ever. And as a veteran fisher of men, Jim Grassi is a reliable guide in this greatest of all adventures.

Having known Jim for over twenty years, I can tell you that he writes from a depth of experience of intentionally investing his life in others that is profoundly rare. Having spent more than forty years discipling others, Jim has proven this is not just a passing interest for him. It is a passion that has become an integral part of his life. And like a skilled guide leading us through treacherous mountain trails, Jim equips his readers with the skills, knowledge, and wisdom necessary to stay on the path charted by our Savior, the greatest Spiritual Mentor the world has ever seen.

With insight, humor, and gripping personal stories, Jim demystifies the frequently intimidating subject of mentorship and helps us gain a fresh vision for how a person can step up and begin to mentor someone else. Within these pages you will discover rich spiritual insights drawn from Scripture, practical tips for countless real-life situations, and time-tested methods for approaching normal, everyday interactions with others in ways that make a lasting difference in someone else's life and legacy.

Don't be fooled: spiritual mentorship is not something to be left to "the professionals." If you know what it means to follow Christ each day just one step at a time, you are ready to begin this adventure. I believe that right now there are colleagues, neighbors, and friends all around you who are desperate for someone to simply share with them the truths and promises that Christ has given to His children.

If you will have the boldness to let Jim be your guide as you begin this adventure, I have no doubt that you will begin to see God work through you in your family, your church, and your community in ways that are astonishing.

So as you prepare to turn the page and begin this journey, get ready to be surprised, and dare to begin this life-changing journey of following in the footsteps of Jesus Christ, the ultimate disciple-maker. You are in good hands. I commend this book and this greatest of adventures to you.

Phil Downer
President, Discipleship Network of America
Author, *Eternal Impact: Investing in the Lives of Others*

INTRODUCTION

Why are discipleship and mentoring so important? What place do they have in our faith? How does discipleship connect to men and the struggles they are facing today? On any given Sunday in most churches across America, men will make up less than 39 percent of the congregation.[1] In Europe, the male makeup of the congregation is much worse, around 5 percent.[2] The most disturbing news suggests that as many as 90 percent of the boys who are being raised in the church will abandon it by their eighteenth birthday. Many of these boys will never return to their faith.[3]

For those precious few who stay in the church, most believe that discipling others is the responsibility of paid professionals—the pastors and missionaries. When we consider the former patriots of the Christian faith, warriors and ambassadors like the apostles Peter or Paul come to mind. After considering world leaders in the discipleship movement like Martin Luther, John Wesley, Charles Finney, A. W. Tozer, Dietrich Bonhoeffer, Charles Spurgeon, Dwight Moody, and Billy Graham, today there seems to be precious few whose primary focus is on discipleship or mentoring. We have many articulate communicators whose Sunday messages inspire people to feel good about themselves, but few are the pastors who preach powerful messages on discipleship that move people to action and to fully commit themselves to the principles of what I call spiritual mentoring. There are some twenty-first-century pastors, teachers, and leaders who consistently speak on and model biblical truths about the primary focus of our faith—discipleship—but their voices are being drowned out amidst the idle chatter of liberal theology and "feel good" religion.

I've had the privilege of serving at Real Life Ministries in Post Falls, Idaho. Pastor Jim Putman, an energetic youth pastor and All-American wrestling coach from Oregon, came to Post Falls fifteen years ago with a heart and vision to share his passion about discipleship and to do church differently. He was a pastor's kid and realized that people were integrating biblical truth into their daily living. Jim realized that hypocrisy was a disease eating like a cancer at the heart of the church.

He and a small team of men came to Post Falls and created some unique models and terminology that are being used by thousands of churches in the nation. I had the privilege of playing a small role in the initial development process, but more importantly, I sat and soaked in much of what Pastor Jim has proclaimed from the pulpit. I've asked Jim that I might include and paraphrase some of that thinking in this work. He and his church are good examples of how God still uses people to connect with others on a one-on-one basis.

We need to revisit what it means to be a true disciple. We need a fresh look at what Christ taught about discipleship. In today's vernacular, first-century discipleship would best be described as *spiritual mentoring*. This book will explain what is needed to rescue our faith and re-purpose our men, and will show how spiritual mentors must play a critical role in bringing the church back to its original purpose. While this work was developed to assist men in knowing God and making Him known, the principles contained within the book are equally transferrable to women and teens.

Despite being critical of those churches that do not embrace a ministry to men as a high priority let's not give up on them. Throughout this work I put forth a positive vision of how to develop a disciple-making ministry which can change the culture of the church. And for those churches empowering their men may God continue to bless and prosper your ministries.

Discipleship is a relational process that requires people to become actively involved in their faith. It is the men who will lead their families back to faith. It is men who can help save the Christian church from the challenges that other religions are placing on our culture. Devoted and active men are the ones who can passionately change the direction of our culture and its destructive patterns that are leading us into chaos and despair. And, most importantly, God has commanded men to be the leaders in the home, church, and community. In discussing the plight of men, psychologist Alexander Mitserlisch stated, "Society has torn the soul of a male, and into this tear the demons have fled—the demons of insecurity, selfishness and despair. Consequently, men do not know who they are as men. Rather, they define themselves by what they do, who they know, or by what they own."[4]

I would agree with that statement, and add that men also define themselves by tasking, duties, and performance. Even when it comes to faith issues, men seem to see their observance of religion by the money they give, the time or work they provide, and the quantity of Scripture they know, instead of a yielded heart given to God.

There is nothing more fundamental to the Christian faith and to building godly men than discipleship. If our mission doesn't include the ingredient of "helping men know God and make Him known," then we have lost the cornerstone of our faith. Is there a greater mission? Once a man intimately knows God through a divine personal relationship with Jesus Christ, then he is directed to "make Him known." Listen to some of Christ's final words to His disciples: "All authority has been given to Me in heaven and on earth. *Go therefore and make disciples of all the nations*, baptizing them in the name of the Father and of the Son and of the Holy Spirit, teaching them to observe all things that I have commanded you; and lo, I am with you always, even to the end of the age" (Matt. 28:18–20, emphasis added).

Theologian Dietrich Bonhoeffer said,

> When Christ calls a man, he bids him come and die. Discipleship means adherence to Christ, and, because Christ is the object of that adherence, it must take the form of discipleship. Christianity without the living Christ is inevitably Christianity without discipleship, and Christianity without discipleship is always Christianity without Christ. Discipleship is "bondage to Jesus Christ alone, completely breaking through every program, every ideal, every set of laws. No other significance is possible, since Jesus is the only significance. Besides Jesus, nothing has significance. He alone matters."[5]

Recurrent themes in Scripture direct us to discipleship. Here are just a few examples:

Matthew 5:16: "Let your light so shine before men, that they may see your good works and glorify your Father in heaven."

Acts 1:8: "You will receive power when the Holy Spirit comes on you. And you will be My witnesses, first here in Jerusalem, then beyond to Judea and Samaria, and finally to the farthest places on earth" (The Voice).

1 Timothy 2:3–4: "For this is good and acceptable in the sight of God our Savior, who desires all men to be saved and to come to the knowledge of the truth."

Romans 10:13–14: "Because *as Scripture says,* "Everyone who calls on the name of the Lord will be saved." How can people invoke His name when they do not believe? How can they believe in Him when they have not heard? How can they hear if there is no one proclaiming Him?" (The Voice).

Romans 1:16: "For I am not ashamed of the gospel of Christ, for it is the power of God to salvation for everyone who believes, for the Jew first and also for the Greek."

Mark 16:15: "Go out into the world and share the good news with all of creation" (The Voice).

The purpose of this book is to help the reader explore and define the topic of discipleship and to make decisions about involvement in this crucial aspect of Christianity. Discipleship is more than attending church on Sunday, writing a check to some missionary, or reading God's Word. Discipleship is much more than communicating information about specific topics. All these things are important, but authentic discipleship is about developing a caring concern and a genuine love for others through modeling Christlike attitudes and behavior in the context of relational environments. We must have a clear biblical definition of discipleship and obey God's commands and plan for our lives within that context.

Biblical discipleship requires a believer to get out of the box of traditional thinking and seek new ways to communicate God's Word and love to a culture that has become hostile to things of the Lord. We need a fresh approach to defining, implementing, and equipping others with a passion to *go make disciples.*

If there is any significant hope in America for the Christian faith, it is with pastors and leaders willing to become true Revolutionaries. According to George Barna, Revolutionaries are "people who are devout followers of Jesus Christ who are serious about their faith, who are constantly worshipping and interacting with God, and whose lives are centered in their belief in Christ."[6] I would add that a revolution cannot occur without true transformation. Individuals who so identify with our Master that we become transformed (changed, altered, and seeking a walk with Jesus that sets them apart from the culture) are the ones who will change our world for the better. If enough men transform their lives, a revival will occur. America has experienced revival before, but it was limited to denominations or specific areas of the country.

If we truly are in the last days before Christ's return, then a global revival will precede His coming. There will be a renewal of our commitment to Christ. Restoration of lives will begin to happen. God will be returned to His rightful place in our society and the people "will turn from their wicked ways." When revival occurs, a Christian revolution can happen.

Because it all starts with the individual, we must see one-on-one discipleship as the primary objective to begin the Revolution. Within the nature of a man is the desire to win battles, identify with important causes, protect his loved ones, and take on hefty goals that are bigger than life itself. The appeal to Christ's followers in the first century was that many men realized it was an "all in" commitment to be a Christian. In his book *Revolution*, George Barna writes:

> They [Revolutionaries] refuse to follow people in ministry leadership positions who cast a personal vision rather than God's, who seek popularity rather than the proclamation of truth in their public statements, or who are more concerned about their own legacy than that of Jesus Christ. Revolutionaries refuse to donate one more dollar to man-made monuments that mark their own achievements and guarantee their place in history. They are unimpressed by accredited degrees and endowed chairs in Christian colleges and seminaries that produce young people incapable of defending the Bible or unwilling to devote their lives to serving others. And Revolutionaries are embarrassed by language that promises Christian love and holiness but turns out to be all sizzle and no substance.[7]

There is no quick fix to the problems of our nation and the decline of interest in the Christian faith. Like a newborn baby, discipling is a life process that begins with care, nurturing, love, and commitment to the responsibilities of being a parent of that child. It requires tremendous dedication, devotion, commitment, and resources to equip a child to be successful in life. So it is with being a true disciple of Jesus. Christ desires each of us to be strong men of character and discipline utilizing the same approach to disciple-making that a good parent brings to raising a child.

What is at stake? It has been said, "As goes the family, so goes the nation." Our government has invested billions of dollars to help shape the educational system and social networks. Our progressive media believes that it is more important to be "politically correct" than to uphold the values of decency and truth. Our social, economic, and political system seems to lack reverence and respect for the biblically based ideals our founding fathers identified in our governing documents.

Can you believe that 41 percent of children will be going to bed this evening in a home with no biological father?[8] When you contemplate this disturbing statistic, it is not a mystery why so many kids are prone to juvenile delinquency, teen pregnancy, sexual identity issues, school difficulties, and more. As never before, we need capable, strong men of God to disciple their kids and to become the spiritual leaders within their families, churches, and communities. One could say, "As goes the husband or father, so goes the family, church, or government." Again, it starts with relationship. Mentoring, discipling, and modeling cannot be replaced by governmental mandates or a social gospel.

And it all starts with you. This book is about challenging you to dig deeper into your faith and convictions. Hopefully you will see some revolutionary ideas and amplified theology on the most important challenge given to mankind by our dear Lord and Savior: "Go make disciples." We have lost our way by listening to slick theological and socially accepted arguments. Too many churches have had their focus on the size of their churches instead of the spiritual depth of their members. If there is a saving grace for the church today, it will be because people like you and me care enough about discipleship that we get out of our complacency and self-centered attitudes and join the most important battle ever fought. We must no longer look at our spiritual development as being something that we "catch" or "fall into," but as an active soldier in the battle for men's souls and for our own.

Through biblical study, metaphors, anecdotes, and practical application, you will find new resources that will help you be a more effective discipler of men. Each chapter will start off with an anecdote that leads to problem identification, followed by some elaboration so you can develop a plan that utilizes the provided Bible studies.

God has pursued man from the beginning of time. His desire is to see men lead and implement His plan for our good. The message needs a messenger. In these last days before our Lord returns God is calling you and me to be that messenger. "How can people invoke His name when they do not believe? How can they believe in Him when they have not heard? How can they hear if there is no one proclaiming Him? (Rom. 10:14 The Voice). Are you that person who will proclaim? If not, why not? The Holy Spirit will equip you, and the biblically based resources contained herein will provide the incentive for you to be a passionate pursuer of men. Will it be easy? No! Nothing worthwhile, least of all the battle for the souls of men, will ever be gained without great effort. Will it be worth it? A resounding yes! Especially when you hear God say, "Well done, good and faithful servant" (Matt. 25:21).

MAN AND THE
CHURCH

For He Himself has said, "I will
never leave you nor forsake you."
—Hebrews 13:5

The following is an excerpt from the journal of my dear
friend and World War II veteran Sgt. Stan Fagerstrom. It brings
to mind the many sacrifices made by those who serve and protect this great country of ours.

I wouldn't walk alone. That thought was uppermost in my
mind as I said goodbye to my companions and turned to start
back down the narrow jungle trail. I had seen too many of my
companions die when we had made our way forward along
that trail. The time was mid-1945.

The place was the jungle high country of central Mindanao in the Philippine Islands. The Japanese had fallen back
along this trail when our forces drove them off the highway
that ran up the middle of the island. They had fallen back
but they hadn't given up. They dug in on higher points along
what we eventually named the "Teardrop Trail." It was well
named.

Those dug in Japanese soldiers waited for us. We never
knew for sure when they would strike. Sometimes they let

half of our company go by. Then bullets tore flesh and you heard brave men cry. We were unable to determine exactly where the fire came from. The thick jungle growth hid our enemy from view.

Many months of jungle combat had taken a toll on my body. My insides finally quit working. My damaged back made it almost impossible for me to keep up. Then came the fever. I just couldn't go on. There was nothing our combat medic could do. "We've got to get you back," the first sergeant said, "but you're going to have to do it on your own. I just don't have anyone to send with you."

He didn't have to say more. I knew what our losses had been. I also knew how close I had come to being among them.

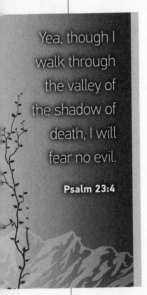

Yea, though I walk through the valley of the shadow of death, I will fear no evil.

Psalm 23:4

But I also knew the sergeant was wrong. I wouldn't have to go back alone. How many miles did I walk back along that jungle trail? Was it five, ten, or fifteen? I don't know. I do know this: Memories of the gut wrenching experiences that had accompanied our advance up that trail haunted every step I took. The trail ran through the slight opening in the jungle where Joe had been hit. Others went down with him. Joe was slow to die. He died pleading for help and with his last words he pleaded for his mother.

We had tried to get to him and in the trying some died. The enemy could see us but we couldn't see them. They were concealed and waiting. Those awful memories came flooding back as I passed by.

Down around the bend was the trail we had left when we attempted to flank the enemy at another spot where we had been hit. Again they were waiting for us. The path we followed in the flank attack was steep. We had moved up but a short distance when they hit us.

My friend Billy was off to the side as I crawled by him. He was holding his left arm. A bullet had torn through his

The battle for men's souls is ultimately one of the key issues for the church today.

left forearm just above the elbow. Before that fight was over we lost several comrades. We couldn't reach their bodies as night began to fall. When we managed to get back the following day their weapons were gone and so was some of their clothing.

I found myself continually choking back tears as I kept moving. But there was no escape from the memories. And then there were spots where those memories were made even stronger. The awful odors seemed to have soaked into those places where the fighting had been intense. We had usually managed to retrieve the bodies of our dead. They were wrapped in a poncho and taken back to battalion headquarters. The bodies of the dead Japanese were often left right where they had fallen.

I crossed the spot where a Japanese soldier had jumped into the foxhole of a sergeant during the night. He killed the sergeant with a knife. The sergeant's swollen body was almost beyond recognition when we had passed by the next morning.

Periodically I paused to check for movement on the trail ahead or behind me. I didn't know how much farther I had to go to reach battalion headquarters. Only my memories of what had happened as we had moved up along it were of help. I knew I was getting closer when I crossed a small jungle stream that crossed the main trail. I knew it wasn't far from battalion headquarters. That stream brought its own memories. Some of our men had died there.

A small advance party from another platoon had taken a break when they found the stream. They welcomed the chance to bathe at least parts of their body, something they'd not done ever since the advance along the trail had started. It was a deadly mistake. The Japanese soldiers concealed in the jungle nearby killed them all. I hadn't seen this happen. I'd been told the Japanese had accomplished their objective using sabers and bayonets. That way there was no gunfire to alert and warn others of us they knew would be coming.

I left the creek and moved on as fast as I could. I moved up another rise in the jungle floor and then there it was—the clearing and our battalion headquarters. I had made it. I knew something else that day. I know it now just as I did then. The first sergeant had been wrong. I hadn't walked that trail alone. Jesus walked with me. I knew He was with me when I took my first step. I knew He would be there if one of those steps turned out to be my last.

Even now, more than half a century later, I find myself asking if I'd have been able to do it had I been all alone. I'm not at all sure that I could have. Second Corinthians says we travel by faith, not by sight.

Sgt. Stan Fagerstrom

WALKING ALONE IS NEVER EASY

No man should have to walk through trials and tribulations alone. Without God in our lives and a good companion to walk with us, life is darn scary. Stan's fears and reflections as he walked along the Teardrop Trail on Mindanao to seek medical help is indicative of the way in which many men see passage through the stress-filled world surrounding their lives. Figuratively speaking, there are the traps of disappointment in the pathways of doing business, snipers with satanic influence to pierce our hearts lurk within the media we view, and too many of our homes are battlefields for couples instead of safe compounds for weary souls.

The significance of the book of Acts as written by the apostle Luke is to enlighten us about the founding of the church, the spread of the gospel, the beginnings of congregations, and the evangelistic efforts in the apostolic pattern (mentoring). In Acts 2:42–44 we read:

> The community continually committed themselves to learning what the apostles taught them, gathering for fellowship, breaking bread, and praying. Everyone felt a sense of awe because the apostles were doing many signs and wonders among them. There was an intense sense of togetherness among all who believed; they shared all their material possessions in trust (The Voice).

What stands out to me was the disciples' love, obedience, encouragement, unity, and focus upon a common vision to *go make disciples.* They truly cared for one another and were committed to their mission. They believed that no person should live life in a vacuum. That is why unity was an important value to these men. Developing unity requires transparency and compassion. This was evident in the first-century church.

We are never too mature to have accountability and fellowship.

Unfortunately, I've met too many men who have simply given up on church. The distractions of competing interests on Sunday have been more attractive than listening to a disconnected and irrelevant message from a stoic pastor. Some men believe that the liberal influences of society have crept into church doctrine, liturgy, and treatment of men, thus eroding its purpose. The feminization of many churches has also put off some guys. Too many sermons seem irrelevant in addressing the issues men face. One guy I spoke with told me that his pastor seemed to only care about his money, service, and membership, and was less interested in helping him work through his heartaches, frustrations, and failures.

The battle for men's souls is ultimately one of the key issues for the church today. I agree with what Dr. Patrick Morley had to say about the battle we face to reach men and the relevancy of the church in today's culture:

> There is raging in the cosmos and all around us a titanic battle between the forces of good and evil for men's souls. . . . The single greatest hope for these men and the world is Christ and His church. I love the church, but the church on the whole has not been able to muster an ongoing will or comprehensive strategy to disciple men. Pastoring men is not a top priority in *any* denomination based upon their actual allocations of financial and intellectual resources.[1]

ARE CHURCHES FAILING TO CONNECT WITH MEN?

If the current church models for developing dynamic discipleship programs are one measure of how effective the church is in reaching men, we would have to submit a failing grade to ourselves. If churches were relevant and intentional about men's issues, we would not be seeing the type of statistics cited by Kent Fillinger: "It is significant that in the average American church there are few conversions, some would say less than 1 baptism per 100 church members."[2]

If the average-sized church in America has two hundred members, it would be fair to assume that 80 percent of the churches in America have only one to two baptisms a year. That means that in most of our nation's churches only one to two people per year are coming into a Christian fellowship and acknowledging their acceptance of Jesus as their Savior. That is pathetic, and it demonstrates clearly that the method of disciple-making isn't working in most churches today. Let's look further at the effectiveness of our current discipleship programs:

* There are approximately 325,000 to 350,000 Christian churches in the United States today.[3]

* There are approximately 247,000,000 Christians in our nation.[4]

* Despite these numbers, it appears that many churches and people are struggling with faith issues.[5]

* In America, 3,500 to 4,000 churches close their doors each year.[6]

* Churches lose an estimated 2,765,000 people each year to nominalism and secularism.[7]

* The average weekly Sunday church attendance has dropped from 1,606,000 in 1968 to 881,000 in 2005.[8]

WHAT ABOUT OUR SENIOR POPULATION?

We can't give up on ourselves or others. Sometimes we will hear older believers say, "I'm just not getting a lot out of church, so I stay home and do church by myself." Isolationism can open the door for temptation, and life without the fellowship found in a church or small group can jeopardize your spiritual health and the intergenerational balance of a church. We are never too mature to have accountability and fellowship. Wade Clark Roof and Sr. Mary Johnson stated:

> "With babes in arms and doubts in mind, a generation looks to religion," is the caption of a *Newsweek* cover story (December 17, 1990) on young Americans returning to God. The post-war "baby boom" generations, having transformed American society in so many ways, is now reshaping the religious landscape. . . . The older boomers are now in their mid-forties and mid-sixties. All together, 75 million strong—roughly one-third of the American population—they are what sociologists called the "lead cohort" of contemporary society, setting trends that include moral values, political attitudes, family life, career patterns, and religions.[9]

Where are these men in our churches? Why aren't they participating more in the winning of souls? I contend that there are reasons this generation is sitting on the bench instead of being active participants (spiritual mentors) in disciple-making.

1. **The church** has failed to properly equip and deploy these men for active service. We have put forth the myth that the "hired guns" (full-time staffers) will do the job. This is wrong thinking!

2. **The men of this generation** were so active in becoming successful that they failed to realize that our legacy is really about being men of significance. Today, these men are

8

seeking a closer relationship with God and want to pass their wisdom on to the following generations.

3. **Many younger pastors** have not asked the older men to get involved in disciple-making (spiritual mentoring) or taught effective messages on how they can. Retired guys sitting home today watching day-time talk shows with their wives could be mentoring students after school or sharing their experiences and cultural values. We could tap this generation to help work with soup kitchens, homeless shelters, church camps, or other places of contact with the younger men. It takes pastors who are confident and not threatened by older men to step up and ask the more mature believers to get involved.

4. **Older men** have been sold a myth that retirement is the end game. There are many retired guys who are very lonely and sad. More mature men need to think about "re-firing," not retiring. Nowhere in Scripture do you see anyone retire. Life after retiring from a vocational career can be the most fulfilling and glorious time in the life of a man. He can actually choose what he wants to do and who he wants to serve. To "re-fire" is to reignite the passion we originally had as a new believer to see others come to know Jesus. Retired men who have walked with Jesus for some time have much to share with others, especially our youth. Many youth today are desiring to have a seasoned male speak into their lives and to learn from their failures and successes.

WHERE IS THE CHURCH?

Rather than looking at the church as a place where we escape the sin of the world, we need to use it to reach those who are *in* the world. It is not uncommon to see new ministries start their services in bowling alleys, motels, theaters, vacant warehouses, mortuaries, and other public gathering places. Often the greatest growth and the time when the church has its greatest impact is during these start-up times.

The ministry formation period requires people to be involved. Chairs and PA systems need to be set up and taken down. Usually snacks, coffee, and other items must be stored and brought from the homes of the members. There is a committee approach to putting the service on, and the members are united around the common vision and goal of reaching new people for Christ.

Unfortunately, once the new property is purchased and the church built, many members feel it's time to turn the operation over to the full-time staff. After the organizational structure is put into place, participation is very often limited to attending service on Sunday morning. Seeking new disciples too often becomes secondary to "putting on the Sunday morning show." In many instances, we see churches become a social gathering place for the saved rather than an equipping center to place people back into the marketplace to meet and encourage those who are broken, confused, and in despair. Pastor Robert Lewis, in his masterful book *The Church of Irresistible Influence*, talks about the need for pastors to be in the marketplace. As I contemplate his work I suggest we consider the following ideas:

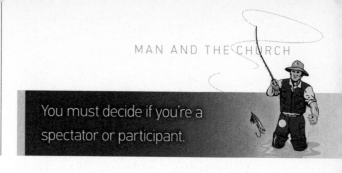

You must decide if you're a spectator or participant.

Our goal as marketplace ministers is to influence those around us for the kingdom of God. To be most effective doing that, we need to be places where unbelievers gather. In business circles, it is not uncommon to be in a hotel where the lounge or bar becomes the place to gather after meeting. . . . The goal is reaching the lost or misguided. Jesus is the perfect role model for this. He was among the people where they lived. He didn't expect them to come to Him; He went to them. He was among sinners and was considered by them as their friend. (See Matthew 11:19.) Yet He remained sinless. He wants us to do the same.[10]

MAYBE THE MESSAGE GOT CONFUSED

It would seem to me that many churches are confused by what Jesus really meant with His command to *go make disciples*. Many modern-day churches seem to believe that discipleship is about "the show," and they display this idea in the design of their buildings, their approach to worship services, and their lack of community involvement. The seeker-sensitive and social gospel approach to mentoring people is often more about entertaining and not offending people than it is about being spiritually honest and truly caring for others.

Jesus said that the gates of hell, the forces of evil in this world, would not be able to stand against His church, not be able to prevent the church from completing its mission of making disciples. Unfortunately, in America today it almost seems as if the powers of evil are prevailing in the lives of men and the ministry of churches. The Devil uses pressure from other cults and religions, the continued spiritual and moral decline of our nation, and the divisions, splits, fights, and feuds within the church today to distract God's people from the all-important work of making disciples.

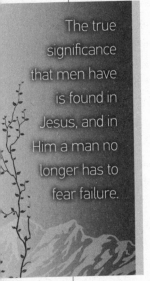

The true significance that men have is found in Jesus, and in Him a man no longer has to fear failure.

You must decide if you're going to fish or cut bait. Will you obey God's command for believers to go and make disciples, or will you merely sit on the sidelines and watch others do the work? Spectators and bait-cutters rarely get to experience the thrill and challenge of the catch. They usually don't take the risk of leaving the shore and confronting the challenges of the sea, facing the risks and costs involved in investing in the lives of others. Being a spectator often leads to being critical of what is happening on the water and evaluating someone else's catch on size or weight, rather than the things that the fisherman had to overcome to catch that particular fish. In a similar manner, some Christians give great weight to a wealthy or powerful person coming to know Christ, instead of being thankful for each and every person who makes a decision. Jesus spent most of His time with the brokenhearted and downcast of society.

Spectators tend to evaluate and determine their comfort level based on what others think or on how the experience or program went. They show emotion while the battles are being fought by others but tend to forget about things once they get back into their daily routines. Their contributions are usually the price of admission and donating to things that directly serve their own interest while watching from the shoreline. Unless asked or pressed, a spectator doesn't utilize his spiritual gifts in ministry or share his testimony with others.

When we first started this ministry a well-known singer and Hollywood personality wrote me a letter. He stated that he and his wife were going to support our ministry because of our approach and earnest desire to reach the unreachable. The man stated that "anyone can fish for Jesus from the safety of the shore but it takes courage and risk to go into the sea of sin and fish for the lost." That was such an encouragement to us that others saw our heart to reach people who might not otherwise come through the front doors of a church.

Participants, on the other hand, are involved in the process. They plan, discover, and deploy the game plan of fishing for men. Yes, dealing with people can lead to frustrations, attacks, and sometimes abandonment. Realistically speaking helping people through tough times and the drama life brings can cause pain, suffering, and unjustified criticism. You can get your clothes smelly and your hands dirty and your hairdo messed up. That is all part of being a fisher of men with Jesus; it is all part of being in the boat with Him versus being a comfortable spectator sitting on the shore who knows neither victory nor defeat because you have failed to become involved.

Too many churches seem focused on slick presentations of the Word without motivating people to apply and deploy what they have heard. I wonder if those who have their ears tickled by "feel-good theology" realize the consequences of not applying what they have heard and read.

THE SPIRITUAL SIDE OF A MAN

Typically, men aren't particularly good when it comes to relationship building, yet this is exactly what God desires of men when He seeks a relationship with them. One of the primary roles of the church is to help facilitate men coming together in a safe and secure environment where they can empty out their baskets of pain, failure, frustration, and disappointment without being judged or condemned. Church needs to be a place where men can talk about their battles with temptations, fear, and depression, while sharing the victories they've had in overcoming the evil one.

> There is tremendous freedom in knowing that because of Christ, men's failures can be forgiven and erased from God's memory.

As an example of how we can create this environment, let's look at the typical men's breakfast. In most churches the relevancy and openness in a men's monthly breakfast is about the same that would be found at a Rotary luncheon. You have a meal, converse around the table about surface issues, and listen to a motivational speaker who doesn't provide specific resources to assist people with any lasting change.

An intentional men's breakfast creates an environment for real change and provides the inspiration and confidentiality that is needed for authentic transformation. It is carefully prayed for and organized so that men know that what they say around a table will not leave the room. Specific discussion questions are provided at the tables where a trained discussion leader helps guide the men to thoughts that begin the process of transformation. The spiritual mentor at each table takes it upon himself to

The church should endeavor to provide opportunities for men to explore and appreciate the spiritual side of their lives.

follow up with the men to explore their issues at a deeper level in a way and environment that is conducive for the struggling participant. My book *Building a Ministry of Spiritual Mentoring* discusses more specifics on how to make this event and other fruitful men-centric endeavors become spiritually fruitful. The bottom line is that the church should endeavor to provide opportunities for men to explore and appreciate the spiritual side of their lives.

Let's define what is meant by developing the spiritual side of a man. Pastor Gary Mortara has aptly defined the relationship God desires to have with men:

> Spiritual, for the purpose here, is a *relationship* with the God of heaven through His Son, the Lord Jesus Christ. Galatians 3:26 says, "You are all children of God through faith in Christ Jesus." When a person comes to God the Father by faith in His Son, the Lord Jesus Christ, God then gives each person the precious gift of the Holy Spirit (See Acts 2:36–38). The Holy Spirit is the internal power source from God. The person of the Holy Spirit is our biggest asset in living a quality, overcoming life. God, who is in heaven, sent His Son (Jesus) to die and pay for the sins of all humanity and then He (Jesus) went back to heaven and is now sitting at the Father's right hand. This is why He has sent the Holy Spirit to come and live within each believer. The Holy Spirit is our teacher. He empowers us and comforts us. The Spirit teaches us the deeper things of God (1 Corinthians 2:10–16)

and leads us from His dwelling within (1 Corinthians 6:19). The Word of God tells us that our confession of "Jesus as Lord" and the belief that God raised Him from the dead, has saved us (Romans 10:9–10). In addition, disciples believe they are Christians, because they have the Holy Spirit who confirms it in our hearts (Romans 8:14).[11]

WHAT IS KEEPING US FROM BIBLICAL DISCIPLESHIP?

In Matthew 16:15–19 we read,

> He said to them, "But who do you say that I am?" Simon Peter answered and said, "You are the Christ, the Son of the living God." Jesus answered and said to him, "Blessed are you, Simon Bar-Jonah, for flesh and blood has not revealed this to you, but My Father who is in heaven. And I also say to you that you are Peter, and on this rock I will build My church, and the gates of Hades shall not prevail against it. And I will give you the keys of the kingdom of heaven, and whatever you bind on earth will be bound in heaven, and whatever you loose on earth will be loosed in heaven."

Jesus said that the gates of hell would not prevail against His church, meaning the forces of evil cannot stop the church from completing its mission of making disciples. Unfortunately, with all the pressure from cults and false religions, the continued spiritual and moral decline, and the divisions, splits, fights, and feuds within the church today, it appears as if Hades is having its way with the American church.

By their nature, most men see themselves as rescuers, protectors, providers, leaders, warriors, and "fixers." Men typically avoid involving themselves in any activity that presents even the

> What will save our nation and Christianity is for believers to band together like the first-century-church and become radical about discipling others.

slightest potential for failure. Men tend to measure life by how successful they are. And, in many cases, being "successful" means steering clear of failure. Thankfully, God values *significance* over *success*. There is tremendous freedom in knowing that because of Christ, men's failures can be forgiven and erased from God's memory. The true significance that men have is found in Jesus, and in Him a man no longer has to fear failure. Someone once said, "Failure is success if we learn from it."

The dynamic tension within men is confusing as they explore "who they are" in comparison to "*Whose* they are." A wise pastor or men's ministry leader will develop strategic opportunities to help men see themselves as their heavenly Father views them. As men grow in God's love and acceptance, they will be transformed from being social or cultural Christians into true disciples of Christ Jesus (Matt. 13:22–23).

IT'S NOT ABOUT THE CHURCH

Jesus didn't tell us to go make a church; He told us to *go make disciples.* We should not be focused upon building big churches, but should focus our efforts upon building spiritually deep disciples. If we build fundamentally strong Christians, then the by-product will be the formation of institutions to bring these people together.

As we analyze biblical prophecy and world events, it would appear that we are entering the end times. As our government continues to seek ways of controlling our faith, it will become increasingly difficult to sustain the megachurch within a culture that will begin to tax church properties, eliminate charitable deductions, and attack the freedom of religion. You add to this dilemma the increased interest and propagation of the Muslim faith and cultic groups, and you have a formula that leads to the continued decline of Christianity.

What will save our nation and Christianity is for believers to band together like the first-century-church and become radical about discipling others. Structure and process can be helpful only as they relate to a one-on-one discipling relationship. Churches that will survive in the twenty-first century are those that place an emphasis on making disciples rather than looking for ways to fund their building projects.

After His resurrection Jesus met with His disciples at the Sea of Galilee. As they enjoyed a fish fry that our Lord put together, Jesus asked His disciples to feed His lambs (young Christians), take care of His sheep (fellow believers), and to feed His sheep (educating and training believers to be both disciples and disciple makers). It is time that we ask church members to take their faith more seriously. Are we truly committed to feeding, educating, encouraging, and discipling His sheep? If we aren't all in, then we must ask ourselves if all we are doing is playing church.

And so we end this chapter where we began. There is a progressive nature to becoming a spiritual mentor who knows God and makes Him known. With the power of the Holy Spirit and some fortitude to face the future, we stand our post and do a good job for our Master Teacher. There will be tests, trials, and many unresolved problems, but we will stand fast and not be fearful. We will fight the good fight, for at the end of our journey we desire to hear those coveted words: "Well done, good and faithful servant; you were faithful over a few things, I will make you ruler over many things. Enter into the joy of your lord" (Matt. 25:21).

BIBLE STUDY

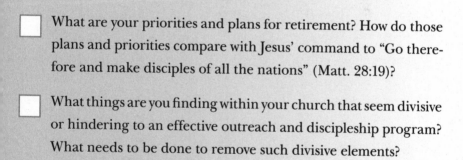

☐ What are your priorities and plans for retirement? How do those plans and priorities compare with Jesus' command to "Go therefore and make disciples of all the nations" (Matt. 28:19)?

☐ What things are you finding within your church that seem divisive or hindering to an effective outreach and discipleship program? What needs to be done to remove such divisive elements?

☐ When was the last time you met with your pastor to discuss how your church and men's group could be more intentional about developing a culture of spiritual mentoring?

MAN
OVERBOARD

> Discipleship is not a question of
> our own doing; it is a matter of making
> room for God so that he can live in us.
>
> **—J. Heinrich Arnold, *Discipleship*[1]**

MAN OVERBOARD

One of my favorite programs on television is the spine-tingling reality series *Deadliest Catch*. On one memorable episode, deckhand Travis was just doing his job on the fishing boat *Trail Blazer* when the cold weather and the high waves knocked him into the icy waters of the Bering Sea. When he hit the water, it was as if a thousand needles had hit all over his body. It looked as though he could not catch his breath. I'm sure his heart was pounding, and he was scared—scared to death. The crew of the *Time Bandit* (which was another crab-fishing boat in the same area) had only a few minutes to pull him out of the water before he would become unconscious and drown. They were also dealing with the possibility that Travis would go into shock and extreme hyperthermia even if they did get him out in time. Through the misty cold air they could hear him screaming, "I don't want to die, get me on board, please get me on board!"

With panic in their hearts and a determination to rescue their fellow fisherman, the crew of the *Time Bandit* moved quickly. They were able to throw Travis a rope that he held on to with every bit of energy he could muster. As he was pulled on board and his body lay shivering on the deck, Travis went into hypothermia, and he temporarily lost his ability to move his arms and legs. Later, however, he sat in the galley muttering his heartfelt thanks to the crew and hugging each one of them—and at that moment Travis began to weep uncontrollably. Later a crew member was overheard saying to the captain, "I wasn't going to let go of him. . . . The last time this happened, we pulled a dead guy out of the water. This time we got him." The courageous crew members, who worked on a different boat than Travis, sacrificed their safety for the life of someone they did not know—and Travis lived because of it.[2]

DRIVENNESS

For many men in contemporary society, there seems to be a "drivenness" about them. Our drive for success often translates into being captive to schedules, demands, and the need for more. Like Travis in our opening story, many men feel as if they are drowning in the waters of debt, competition, and despair that have been brought about by their own push for success, rather than their relying on Christ for guidance and strength.

Jonah appears to have been a driven person with lofty goals and a plan that wasn't connected to what God wanted him to do. The Lord commanded him to go to Nineveh to preach against

Many men feel they are drowning in the waters of debt, competition, and despair. There is a life preserver—it's Jesus.

the nation's great wickedness, but Jonah did just the opposite: he jumped aboard a ship that was heading for a different city in a different direction. Jonah's plans for the future did not include leading the nation of Nineveh to repentance, so he tried to set his own plans ahead of God's.

Like Jonah, when we try to place our plans in front of God's will, we can find ourselves in a heap of trouble. We get into trouble when we fail to recognize that God is with us always. Jesus reminded His disciples of this when He gave them the Great Commission: "And lo, I am with you always, even to the end of the age" (Matt. 28:20). Nothing escapes His notice, but much escapes *our* notice. Our awareness of His presence often falters or fades as we are consumed with distractions and interruptions that take our focus off of Him. Our lives are so fragmented and our focus is on our problems that prayer and fellowship with God is lost in the shuffle. But when we make time to narrow our focus on things of the Lord, we find that life's journey goes much smoother.

TRAITS OF DRIVEN MEN

There is a profound difference between being a driven, self-guided man, and being a Spirit-guided man. Men who are driven and self-guided will frequently exhibit some or all of the following traits:

Men are tired. Most men struggle by trying to put twenty pounds of expectations and activities into a ten-pound bag. The tyranny of the urgent has created much stress for many men. They are exhausted, stressed, fatigued, slammed, and weary of the numerous duties and responsibilities Christian men experience.

Men lack biblical balance in their lives. "When I relax, I feel guilty," is a confession many men make. Men find it hard to balance all the demands life puts on them. This country's complex social and economic system allows little personal time for meditation, relaxation, and restoration.

Many men are depressed. In his book *Blue Genes*, Paul Meier wrote: "Upon reflection, men generally believe they could have done a better job as a husband and father. No amount of fame, fortune, or worldly success can ever be enough to compensate for failures at home."[3] Approximately 30 percent of the participants in our men's retreats and conferences acknowledge suffering from clinical symptoms of depression.

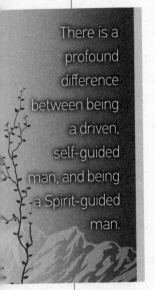

There is a profound difference between being a driven, self-guided man, and being a Spirit-guided man.

Most driven men are loners. Busy men often claim that they have no time for relationships or accountability groups. Many loners pay the price for their isolation by finding themselves ensnared in pornography, affairs, or other destructive addictions. Driven men need to love and be loved—and that takes time. There's no shortcut to building healthy, lasting relationships.

Driven men often equate success with the acquisition of stuff. God hasn't called us to live by worldly standards. Earthly idols (e.g., money, titles, position, material possessions, beautiful homes, sports, hobbies, the praise of men, the attainment of superior intelligence, etc.) will never fulfill

> Driven men need to love and be loved, and that takes time. There's no shortcut to building healthy, lasting relationships.

man's God-given need for significance. In Ecclesiastes 2:11 King Solomon ultimately came to the conclusion that, after a lifetime of chasing after the things of this world, everything under the sun was nothing more than vanity, dust, and wind.

What is it that men need and want? If men desire to be Spirit-filled and Spirit-led disciples, then what are some of the voids we need to recognize?

WHAT DO MEN WANT MOST?

Dr. Pat Morley and his *Man in the Mirror* organization have provided many resources that have inspired those of us involved in ministry to men. The following are observations formed from our collective research. First and foremost, give men what they *need* in the context of what they *want*, delivered in a system that *produces results*, and you will have accomplished much. Many men's ministry leaders state that men want

* A *cause* that they can give their lives to that will make a difference—a mission that has significance, meaning, and purpose

* A *companion* to share it with—relationships, love, wife, family, friends, and acceptance

25

* A *conviction* that gives a reasonable explanation for why numbers 1 and 2 are so different—a belief system, worldview, philosophy, or religion[4]

To this list I would add:

* A *communication system* that helps them become more transparent and open to understand their loved ones and associates—words and actions that transmit a blessing to others

* A *common goal* that binds like-hearted men together—vision, business plan, and strategies that bring men together for experience, action, and growth

* A *church* that is real and connected to their souls. Pastors and congregations who see men in light of their passions, interests, problems, and concerns are very much needed. Men need places where burdens are unloaded, hope is provided, and grace is given.

* A *Christian experience* where the fruit of the Spirit and joys of their faith can be felt through an understanding that these rewards are only found when men are willing to suffer with Christ through self-denial, obedience, testing, self-sacrifice, and surrender.

* A group of *partners* who will surround them with unconditional love and support—willing to "watch their backs," tell them the truth in a loving way, and model Christ's love in a way that helps them feel protected and safe even when the walls of life come tumbling down around them.

✳ A *wife and family* that provide a supportive environment where men can become renewed and restored. Men thrive in an environment of love and mutual respect. In the end, one of the most cherished things any man can ever experience is knowing that his family respects him.

TRANSFORMATION OF THE CARNAL MAN

What is it that a mature Christian can do to help our brothers find the joy and peace in their lives that transform them into the likeness of Christ? The carnal nature of every man wants to rule. We have such difficulty letting go and letting God. By our nature we are fix-it people. Problems and challenges are inescapable and woven into the very fabric of this fallen world. In an age when independence is king, we find it hard to acknowledge that we really can't do it by ourselves. In addition to all those things, we tend to weigh ourselves down with burdens and responsibilities that are above our pay grade. The reality is that we are limited in correcting all the misery and injustices in the world today.

We need to seek God's perspective on things and give to Him those things that seem insurmountable. The prophet Isaiah helps us get this into perspective: "The LORD will guide you continually, and satisfy your soul in drought, and strengthen your bones; you shall be like a watered garden, and like a spring of water, whose waters do not fail" (Isa. 58:11).

If we agree that discipleship is fundamental to our faith—and if we also agree that being an effective disciple is not primarily about structure, strategy, institution, or program, but about relationship—then the carnal man needs to be transformed from thinking about the process to thinking about developing caring, loving, and considerate relationships that model and encourage people to seek God's kingdom.

REAL TRANSFORMATION: HEAD TO HEART TO HANDS

A good workbook on discipleship comes to us from Real Life Ministries in Post Falls, Idaho. For years the pastors at Real Life have taught some principles on spiritual growth that help us understand the essence of change. The following is my paraphrase of the material.

A DISCIPLE'S HEAD

When Jesus said to His disciples, "Follow Me, and I will make you fishers of men" (Matt. 4:19), He intended that, through the power of the Holy Spirit, changes would be made in His followers. A decision to follow Jesus is a head-level decision that, through knowledge and the leading of the Spirit, one seeks to know Christ. A disciple makes a decision to follow and know Jesus, the living God. This happens by accepting who He is, what He did for our salvation, and why we need His comforting Spirit to live a life of significance. Knowing Jesus is really the first step in the process of becoming a believer. In John 1 we read that the disciples came to know Him by spending time with Him. Spending time with Him through prayer and studying His Word changes our motives, attitudes, and actions.

It is at the head level that knowledge is gathered. In the *Eerdmans Bible Dictionary* we find a great definition of knowledge: "Knowledge in the Old Testament connotes an intimate

The carnal nature of every man wants to rule.

acquaintance with something. This is not so much knowledge 'about,' in the sense of an objective, mental apprehension. Rather, a personal relationship is implied between an individual and the object, whether a spiritual relationship as between worshipper and deity (Ps. 135:5; Isa. 1:2–3; Hos. 5:3), a social relationship between two people (Gen. 29:5), or sexual relationship between husband and wife (4:1; 1 Samuel 1:19)."[5]

A DISCIPLE'S HEART

To be a disciple means that head knowledge of Christ moves toward the heart. If we truly desire to be like Him, then our knowledge must begin to translate into change from within. Our character, attitudes, priorities, and hearts testify that our actions of loving God and loving others are palpable. The Holy Spirit helps to make us into relational people with an eternal perspective in mind. When we desire to be like Christ and to mimic His love, care, and compassion, then there is evidence that something new is in our hearts and souls. This change is a supernatural thing that is empowered by being filled with His Spirit.

Discipleship is a heart-oriented process of change that occurs when we enter into a relationship with Jesus. The fishermen were called to leave their nets, leaving something tangible behind; similarly, we are called to leave behind our old lives. Instead of living a life for self, we need to begin thinking of God and others. Instead of being consumed with worldly desires and lusts, we need to take up our cross and follow Him.

It is amazing how God will replace those things in our lives that brought us excitement and fun from a worldly perspective. God asks us to abandon those things that erode our relationship with Him. As a holy and just God, He seeks to have relationship with us, but our sinful natures stand in the way. Indulging in ungodly things takes our focus and attitudes off the promises God has for us.

To be a disciple means that head knowledge of Christ moves toward the heart.

Following Jesus could also be called losing our lives in the sense that we are "dying to self." It is in giving our lives to God's plan and purpose that we find true peace, comfort, and joy. God wants to give us the desires of our hearts, just as a good father wishes the best for his children (Ps. 20:4).

While salvation is free, discipleship has its cost. "If anyone desires to come after Me, let him deny himself, and take up his cross daily, and follow Me. For whoever desires to save his life will lose it, but whoever loses his life for My sake will save it. For what profit is it to a man if he gains the whole world, and is himself destroyed or lost? For whoever is ashamed of Me and My words, of him the Son of Man will be ashamed when He comes in His own glory, and in His Father's, and of the holy angels" (Luke 9:23–26).

A DISCIPLE'S HANDS

When we really know Christ and begin the process of a heart transformation, we will see how God wishes to use our hands. We suddenly become interested in *fishing for men*. Most often fishing for men involves connecting with guys through acts of service, works of kindness, spending time with others, and using our gifts, abilities, talents, and learned skills to develop relationship with others.

It has been said that people don't care about how much you know until they know how much you care. Think about it. If we want to build a relationship with another man, it most often starts with something like:

* helping him work on a project around his house

* lending him a tool or piece of equipment

* taking him to a game

* enjoying together a hobby like golf, fishing, hunting, or bicycling

* showing care and concern for his family

* inviting them over for dinner

* meeting him at his workplace to see what he does

* joining a service organization

* serving within the community at a soup kitchen or volunteering with the police department

* serving at a nursing home or retirement center

* going on a missions trip

The list is as varied as there are interest areas, gifts, and talents.

When a person meets Christ, his life is transformed into a practical mission that involves connecting with others. A disciple studies ways he can relate to others by understanding the way they are wired, as well as their passions, interests, fears, and frustrations. Initially, this happens best in informal settings and by using your imagination to intentionally care about and love others. Jesus met people where they were and didn't expect them to come to the synagogue with Him. What are you doing to meet new people who are broken and lost?

Some readers will say, "I don't have the time." Who is it that took the time to introduce you to Christ? Jesus modeled the transformation process within the context of everyday life. It was part of how He operated. He encourages us to begin making disciples wherever we go. Help move the person you want to disciple into your friendships and areas of interest first. The Bible-thumping approach to reaching people for Christ rarely works in today's culture. People first need to know that you really care, that you won't condemn, that you will encourage them with a vision of hope and love, and that you will walk with them through the discipleship process.[6]

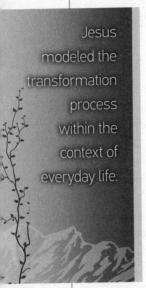

Jesus modeled the transformation process within the context of everyday life.

Christ discipled people by being with them, even with people whom His society and culture viewed as outcasts, such as a woman He met in Samaria. "Now Jacob's well was there [in Samaria]. Jesus therefore, being wearied from His journey, sat thus by the well. It was about the sixth hour. A woman of Samaria came to draw water. Jesus said to her, 'Give Me a drink'" (John 4:6–7). Notice what Jesus did in this passage: He was weary from travel, but rather than find an inn or a place for the night, He deliberately sat down in a very public place where He knew He would be meeting strangers. It was considered "defiling" in Jesus' day for a Jew to speak with a Samaritan—and this

Christ discipled people by being with them, even with people whom His society and culture viewed as outcasts.

went double for a Jewish man to be speaking with a Samaritan woman—yet Jesus did not hold back. He immediately struck up a conversation, and He chose a topic where the woman could not simply make small talk. She was there specifically to draw water, so He asked her to share that water with Him.

Sometimes the Lord calls us to approach people whom we might feel a natural disinclination toward, people we would not ordinarily choose to spend time with. But we can bridge those gaps by offering to work together on some common task, such as Jesus did when He asked the woman to share water. Who at work, at school, or within your network isn't particularly easy to be with? What could you do to build a relational bridge to those people?

Christ taught people by providing practical examples. He regularly used examples, metaphors, similes, paradoxes, proverbs, and real-life situations to show them something. After sharing the Last Supper with His disciples, Jesus stood up and did something that utterly shocked His friends. "Jesus, knowing that the Father had given all things into His hands, and that He had come from God and was going to God, rose from supper and laid aside His garments, took a towel and girded Himself" (John 13:3–4). Notice His motivation: He bowed Himself before His disciples and washed their feet, *because He is God!* Our human, worldly wisdom would say that this was the most compelling reason *not* to bow before the feet of another, but Jesus wanted to teach His disciples to humble themselves and serve one another. He didn't just preach to them; He taught by powerful example. While it is an over-used expression, it is still true: more is caught than taught.

Christ demonstrated God's love by His acts of kindness. Jesus didn't come to be judgmental or critical, but through touch, spoken words of encouragement, and acts of generosity He portrayed the love of God, such as when He healed the blind man (John 9). What practical demonstration of service could you do that would speak volumes to someone about Christ's love? Maybe there is a neighbor who needs to see an act of kindness (e.g., raking their lawn, snow blowing their driveway, taking some trash to the dump).

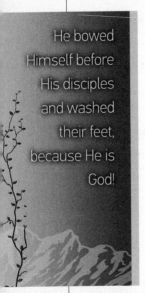

He bowed Himself before His disciples and washed their feet, because He is God!

Christ was realistic and direct. Jesus talked to people about everyday life and things that impacted them. In the Sermon on the Mount, He spoke about worry, lust, divorce, prayer, and money. Are your conversations with unsaved people too theological, or do they reflect real-life situations that impact others?

Christ teaches us about growing in our faith. Jesus regularly prayed and discussed with His disciples the importance of taking time to know God. The apostle Peter reminds us to "grow in the grace and knowledge of our Lord and Savior Jesus Christ" (2 Peter 3:18). How much time do you spend daily in prayer, Bible study, and meditation? How can we know God's plan for our lives if we don't listen to what He has to say?

Christ taught His disciples to empty self and to be filled with the Holy Spirit, the Comforter (Acts 1:5, 8; 2 Cor. 1:4). As we fill ourselves with His Word, love, compassion, and presence, the ugly part of our worldly nature disappears. Imagine a transparent mannequin with a deflated colored balloon on the inside that can be expanded into the same shape and size as the model. As the inner colored balloon (Christ-like life) is filled with air (Holy Spirit), it pushes the old air (worldly nature) out and the colored balloon fills in the void. So it is with our Spirit-filled lives. The more Christ takes over our body, mind, and spirit, the more the old nature is squeezed out and the new nature fills the void.

Practically speaking, if we continue to live in sin, hang out with the same people who tempt us, or maintain the same behaviors that lead us away from Christ, we are trying to walk in both the natural and spiritual worlds. The apostle Paul reminds us, "I say then: Walk in the Spirit, and you shall not fulfill the lust of the flesh. For the flesh lusts against the Spirit, and the Spirit against the flesh; and these are contrary to one another, so that you do not do the things that you wish. But if you are led by the Spirit, you are not under the law" (Gal. 5:16–18). And in John 14:26 we read, "But the Helper, the Holy Spirit, whom the Father will send in My name, He will teach you all things, and bring to your remembrance all things that I said to you."

YOUR SPIRITUAL EPITAPH

When Jesus commanded His disciples to count the cost of discipleship, He was effectively asking them to consider what their epitaph might be, what memorial words might be written on their gravestone. This is intended to be a short but precise description of a man's life—not from the perspective of the man who died, but from the perspective of those who knew him best.

When his friends and family looked at his life, what sort of man did they see?

This is a very important question that all disciples must ask themselves: How do I want Jesus to summarize my life? Personally, I want to hear Him say, "Well done, good and faithful servant" (Matt. 25:21); I want to know that I fulfilled the Father's will in my lifetime. The epitaph that you want to have written about your life will reveal your deepest heart's desires; it will define what your most important goals are in your life at present.

Let us end this section with a quote from Bob Buford:

> Saint Augustine said that asking yourself the question of your own legacy—*What do I wish to be remembered for?*—is the beginning of adulthood. That is what I have done by writing my own epitaph. After all, an epitaph should be something more than a wispy, wishful, self-selected motto. If it's honest, it says something about who you are at the essence of your personality and your soul. . . .
>
> The parable of the sower gets to the center of my dreams and to the kernel of my experiences. It is the driving force behind this book. My passion is to multiply all that God has given me, and in the process, give it back. . . .
>
> If the first half was a quest for success, the second half is a journey to significance.[7]

BIBLE STUDY

If anyone comes to Me and does not hate his father and mother, wife and children, brothers and sisters, yes, and his own life also, he cannot be My disciple. And whoever does not bear his cross and come after Me cannot be My disciple. For which of you, intending to build a tower, does not sit down first and count the cost, whether he has enough to finish it—lest, after he has laid the foundation, and is not able to finish, all who see it begin to mock him, saying, "This man began to build and was not able to finish." Or what king, going to make war against another king, does not sit down first and consider whether he is able with ten thousand to meet him who comes against him with twenty thousand? Or else, while the other is still a great way off, he sends a delegation and asks conditions of peace. So likewise, whoever of you does not forsake all that he has cannot be My disciple. (Luke 14:26–33)

☐ What are the costs of discipleship that Jesus lays out in this passage?

☐ What did He mean when He said that a disciple must "hate his father and mother, wife and children, brothers and sisters, yes, and his own life also" (v. 26)?

☐ What did Jesus mean when He said, "whoever does not bear his cross and come after Me cannot be My disciple" (v. 27)?

☐ How much cost are you prepared to pay to be a disciple of Christ?

MENTORING
MEN FOR THE
MASTER

A disciple is a person-in-process
who is eager to learn and apply the
truths that Jesus Christ teaches him,
which will result in ever-deepening
commitments to a Christ-like lifestyle.

—**Christopher B. Adsit,**
Personal Disciple-Making[1]

MOTIVATOR AND MENTOR

I've had the privilege of being at several NFL training camps
and observing various coaches. Their personalities, techniques,
and experiences vary, but their passion, commitment, and dedication for the game and to the players is profound. One of the
coaches I really enjoyed watching was former Oakland Raiders
head coach Jon Gruden. The drive, passion, and determination
you see on television is exactly what he was like on the practice
field.

His persona was a unique mix of Coach Bill Walsh, motivational speaker Zig Ziglar, encourager Reverend Norman Vincent

Peale, and rock star Bruce Springsteen. It truly was inspirational just to watch Jon in action. One second he would be joking with a guy, only to shift gears into telling another player that if he didn't get his head in the game then he should go home and take a shower.

As Gruden was one of the youngest guys ever to be hired as an NFL head coach, the players loved him and seemed to connect with his philosophy. Since he was athletic and young enough to keep up with the guys, periodically during a practice session you would see him leave the sideline, fold up his notes, tuck them in his pants, and go out on the field to play a position as a defensive back or wide receiver. If a player wasn't catching on to how to do his job, Jon would show him. He modeled his teachings.

Not only was Jon an extraordinary motivator, but he was also a good mentor to the coaching staff and players. He even made time in his busy schedule to listen to this old chaplain as I tried to encourage him. His ability to mentor people has been captured in ESPN's very popular program *Jon Gruden's Quarterback Camp.*

WHO WILL MENTOR THE MEN?

Convincing men that mentoring works and is essential to the Christian faith is a key problem for the Christian church. If a young man doesn't have a biblical role model at home, where is he going to find the truths and foundational principles that will help him become a man of significance? It won't be taught to him in our schools, colleges, and universities. He probably can't find it in a thirty-minute message taught from a pulpit, given the fact that most Christian men attend church only three times

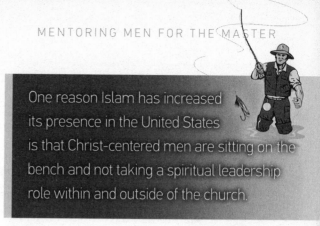

One reason Islam has increased its presence in the United States is that Christ-centered men are sitting on the bench and not taking a spiritual leadership role within and outside of the church.

every two months. The media won't be a resource, as it has totally distorted the role of a man and the traditional values and beliefs of our faith. Who will help a man take a stand on character and help him hold to his convictions? It must be another godly man who will model Christ-like character through a discipling environment.

There is a void in godly male leadership in this country. If Christian men don't rise up and start a spiritual revolution to sustain the faith, then who will? One reason Islam has increased its presence in the United States is that Christ-centered men are sitting on the bench and not taking a spiritual leadership role within and outside of the church.

Jesus told us, "For everyone to whom much is given, from him much will be required; and to whom much has been committed, of him they will ask the more" (Luke 12:48). You might be saying to yourself, "What have I been given? What has been committed to me?" But if you are a born-again follower of Jesus Christ, then you need to recognize that *very much* indeed has been given to you! You have been given eternal life; you have been given forgiveness for every sin you will ever commit in your life; much more than these, you have been given the presence of the Holy Spirit in your own life! The very presence of God in your life means that much has been committed to you: the spreading of the gospel so that others might gain the priceless gifts you've been given; mentoring and training and discipling other men so that they might come to understand that much has been committed to them as well. Much has been given to you, Jesus said, and therefore He expects much in return.

> The very presence of God in your life means that much has been committed to you.

There was a man named Ananias who recognized this important principle. He was a mature man of faith in the early Christian church, and the Lord told him in a dream that he needed to seek out a man named Saul and heal him of blindness—despite the fact that Saul was well-known as a persecutor and murderer of Christians! Yet Ananias obeyed the Lord because he knew that much was required of him. This Saul, of course, was the apostle Paul, but it took a long time before he was recognized and trusted by the other disciples of Christ. At one point Paul had to flee to Jerusalem to avoid being killed, but when he tried to join the disciples there, he discovered that they were afraid of him and wanted nothing to do with him! Fortunately, however, a man named Barnabas understood that he had been given much, so he was not afraid when much was required of him, and he stepped forward and took Paul under his wing. These men all understood that they would be called upon by God to do great things simply because they had already been *given* great things.

We grow and become wiser because someone has invested in us, and we in turn invest in others. Some will say, "Well, I don't feel qualified to mentor someone else." The way God will mold and shape your life is when you empty self through prayer, study, reflection, and obedience, applying what you know in a relational environment to someone who is struggling with life.

Like Ananias and Barnabas, Paul also came to understand that he had been given much through Christ and that he had a responsibility to give much to others, just as others had done for him. He discipled many young men including Timothy, to whom he wrote two important New Testament epistles. Thus it was that he was able to exhort the believers in Corinth to imitate his example: "Therefore, whether you eat or drink, or whatever you do, do all to the glory of God. Give no offense, either to the Jews or to the Greeks or to the church of God, just as I also please all men in all things, not seeking my own profit, but the profit of many, that they may be saved. Imitate me, just as I also imitate Christ" (1 Cor. 10:31–11:1). This imitation is exactly what discipleship is all about.

MENTOR OR DISCIPLER?

Coach Gruden was indeed a mentor to his players. He didn't just focus on the athletic pursuits of his players; he also cared about each man's character development and relationships with other players. Gruden made it a practice to care about a player both on and off the field. He would often call guys into his office to help work out personal issues so that distractions would be eliminated and a player could focus on his job. Coach Gruden was a mentor because he became a trusted adviser, counselor, teacher, and guide to the men on his team.

In the purest sense, discipling a person suggests that you are focused upon the spiritual development of an individual. Discipling a person is helping that person become Christ-like in his motives, attitudes, and daily living. Pat Morley gave a good working definition of a disciple in his book *Pastoring Men*: "A disciple is someone *called* to live 'in' Christ, *equipped* to live 'like' Christ, and *sent* to live 'for' Christ."[2] Thus a discipler is a person who will help equip the disciple to become more like Christ so he in turn can disciple others.

Mentoring and discipleship are very similar, and you will find in this book that I use the terms interchangeably; however, the essence of discipleship is finding a spiritual mentor with whom you can connect. I like the term *spiritual mentoring*. It implies the heart of discipling another person within the context of a relational mentoring environment. That is to say, the most effective and long-lasting discipling relationships happen best when you seek to encourage and equip the person in areas beyond just the spiritual aspects of life. If you can find common interest areas such as sports, hobbies, cultural interests, work, or family, your relationship will have dimensions that will help hold you together during trying times.

During the time of Christ, a spiritual teacher or mentor was called a *didaskalos* (Luke 2:46). Jewish teachers taught through the use of a discipleship process, allowing the students to ask questions to which the teacher would reply. They did not have any official position and received no salary. These teachers were common men who cared enough about others to share their lives and experiences to help others deal with life.

I define a spiritual mentor as someone who disciples another through the use of relational platforms so as to fully connect with the person being mentored. Being a spiritual mentor is ultimately about building a relationship that can help both parties become stronger in their faith. If we agree that the most precious of gifts is *time*, then the idea of investing in others or having someone invest in you is a special thing.[3]

Solomon has provided us some important insight into the importance of mentoring relationships: "Two are better than one, because they have a good reward for their labor. For if they fall, one will lift up his companion. But woe to him who is alone when he falls, for he has no one to help him up. Again, if two lie down together, they will keep warm; but how can one be warm alone? Though one may be overpowered by another, two can withstand him. And a threefold cord is not quickly broken" (Eccl. 4:9–12). Notice that these principles apply equally to the mentor and to the one being discipled. The mentoring relationship between two men strengthens *both* men; the accountability and friendship and selflessness work both ways, helping the mentor to stay strong in the Lord just as much as it helps the one being mentored.

The reality is that more guys want to be mentored than there are mentors to go around.

One of the reasons more males die of heart attacks than women is that men want to deny that anything is wrong. It is common for men to feel that they can tough it out or keep strong, as though it were "sappy" to build a godly and deep relationship with another man. Sociologists at Duke and the University of Arizona found that, on average, most adults only have two people they can talk to about the most important subjects in their lives such as serious health problems or who will care for their children should they die. And about 25 percent of those surveyed had not one close friend.[4] The reality is that more guys want to be mentored than there are mentors to go around. It can be difficult finding a mentor because in today's hectic world many guys just don't have the time. And there are those men who don't feel they are spiritually mature enough to disciple someone or to offer something of value.

One of the key things that young guys between fifteen and thirty years of age are looking for in the older generation is a real friend who will listen and share life experiences. According to the U.S. Census, 41 percent of kids in America will go to bed tonight in a household where no biological father exists.[5] The problems of divorce and unmarried mothers trying to raise a young man are becoming epidemic, and this phenomenon is part of the reason why more men are growing up in isolation. We need spiritual mentors, true disciples, to reach out and encourage young men in things of the Lord.

FINDING A BARNABAS, PAUL, OR TIMOTHY

It might seem daunting at first to find someone to be your Barnabas or your Timothy, someone to mentor you or someone for you to mentor. Use the following principles to get started, and depend upon the Lord to lead you together with the right man.

Fairly assess yourself: It is important that you understand yourself, your expectations, and your needs so you can be of good counsel to others. A disciple also needs clarification on the same issues so that he can effectively select the right spiritual mentor. Once again, it's the apostle Paul who gives us insight on this issue: "Because of the grace allotted to me, I can *respectfully* tell you not to think of yourselves as being more important than you are; devote your minds to sound judgment since God has assigned to each of us a measure of faith" (Rom. 12:3 The Voice). We need to see ourselves the way that God sees us. And it is no coincidence that this verse follows Paul's exhortation that all believers must "not allow this world to mold you in its own image. Instead, be transformed *from the inside out* by renewing your mind. As a result, you will be able to discern what God wills and whatever God finds good, pleasing, and complete" (v. 2 The Voice). In other words, we can only gain a correct perspective on ourselves by first renewing our minds to think the way that God thinks. Analyze your gifts, talents, personality, temperament, experiences, and spiritual depth, as well as the type of people you are drawn to or trust. Once you understand who you are, then think about the type of person you would listen to or who would best challenge you to grow deeper in your faith.

> We can only gain a correct perspective on ourselves by first renewing our minds to think the way that God thinks.

Pray: Don't rely on your own wisdom; seek the Lord's wisdom. Submit to God what you know about yourself and ask Him to direct and guide you to someone who will best connect with you. Once the Lord brings someone to mind, ask that person to pray about the discipling relationship. Fear will grip you because it is uncommon for men to reach out in this intimate way to other men, but allow the Holy Spirit to work in the other man's heart as well as your own. If you are looking for a man to be your mentor, identify a short list of men who you think are more mature in the things of God than you are. Then you can begin to ask them if they would take the time and be willing to begin a spiritual journey with you. Don't let a "no" answer shut you down. People are very busy and some guys just don't feel worthy. Prayer should open and close each time you meet.

Avoid overload: Don't overload your mentor or disciple with too many questions, details, or information as you begin the relationship. A good spiritual mentor isn't called to disciple someone because he is expected to "fix" the person. That is God's job. Spiritual mentors spend as much or more time listening and reflecting as they do sharing examples or suggesting areas of personal growth. The spiritual mentor needs to allow God to do His work through the Holy Spirit preparing the disciple's heart for change. The spiritual mentor's responsibility is to provide the environment for spiritual growth, not to cause the growth. And always remember that God uses the entire body of Christ to do His work. As Paul reminds us, "I planted, Apollos watered, but God gave the increase. So then neither he who plants is anything, nor he who waters, but God who gives the increase" (1 Cor. 3:6–7).

Utilize resources: Find a Bible study or good Christian book to help direct your initial conversation. Most men, unless they are totally broken, tend not to share intimate details about their life until trust is built and a real connection is made. Keep your conversations and ideas real and genuine. Don't try to impress someone or present an unreal image of yourself. If transformational growth is to happen, then honest and accurate communications need to happen.

Cultivate relational environments: Seek to have fellowship around a meal or cup of coffee. Informal settings like fishing, hunting, or golf are also good ways to create a relational environment that is conducive to fruitful and open discussions. Relational environments help build trust and openness. When

> The spiritual mentor needs to allow God to do His work through the Holy Spirit preparing the disciple's heart for change. The spiritual mentor's responsibility is to provide the environment for spiritual growth, not to cause the growth.

you work together on projects or excursions, and when you share adventures, bonds are built.

Keep to your schedule: Be consistent in where and when you meet. The more you meet, the faster and deeper your relationship will grow. Be respectful of each other's schedules, but be firm about being regular in your time together. Agree to try the relationship for at least three months so each of you has an opportunity to evaluate the value of the experience. Remember, except for Jesus, nothing is forever. A good time to end a discipling relationship is when the person you are mentoring is ready to mentor someone else. You might find that your relationship with another guy addresses a season of time for each of you, then it's time to move on to another relationship. Also remember that when you dive into a relationship there will be some pain and at times discomfort. That is the nature of being real and moving forward with a forgiving spirit. Any relationship worth having may at times feel awkward, and misunderstandings sometimes occur. It is when you work through these things that people are tested and grow closer together and trust is built.

Maintain accountability: Accountability helps men get to the heart of the issues they face. By developing an honest and forthright relationship, it is fair that you begin a process of personal discovery and accountability on matters that help keep people focused on God's purpose and plan for our lives. For example, pornography is a big temptation in our culture today. It is important that the spiritual mentor and person being discipled feel they can ask one another questions that deal with time spent on watching or participating in pornography, as well as countless other topics that might be of importance to both men.

Care: A good spiritual mentor is also a caring and compassionate person. He looks for opportunities to show

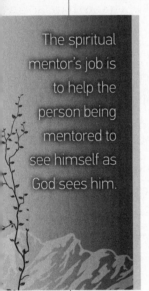

The spiritual mentor's job is to help the person being mentored to see himself as God sees him.

Christ's love in tangible ways. By letting a person know you are praying for him or offering to help him with a problem, you will testify clearly that you care enough to address his concerns. One thing that really demonstrates your concern is when you do something for the other man's family. If you can show genuine love and care for his kids, then you will automatically get his attention. When you care for others and really get close to them, expect that you can occasionally be misunderstood or attacked. We live in a broken world, and some people will recoil and revert to attacking others when they feel you are too close to knowing the truth about their lives. This has happened to me many times over. Just hang in there and show them that, like Jesus, despite their sin you love and accept how God made them.

Pursue justice: Be fair and balanced in your assessment and comments. If a man is already discouraged, broken, hurting, and beaten down, it would not be advisable to place more guilt and shame on his shoulders. He needs a friend who will be an encourager and who will speak the truth in love. Scripture reminds us that "we will no longer be like children, tossed around here and there upon ocean waves, picked up by every gust of religious teaching spoken by liars or swindlers or deceivers. Instead, by truth spoken in love, we are to grow in every way into Him—the Anointed One, the head" (Eph. 4:14–15 The Voice).

Notice that Paul expects two things from us who "will no longer be like children": speak the truth, but do so in love. Pursuit of justice requires both: we need to be willing to speak the truth, addressing areas of sin or weakness in one another that need to be addressed, but we also need to do so out of a pure motivation of genuine love and concern for one another. Only by doing both, Paul teaches, can we hope to grow up into Christ.

Remember that your goal is to help the other man develop a lifelong relationship with the living God. The spiritual mentor's job is to help the person being mentored to see himself as God sees him (Rom. 12). By carefully listening and asking penetrating questions, you can help the person see the blind spots in his life and where the Holy Spirit would have him change.

Protect confidentiality: Confidentiality is key to a successful discipling experience. "What happens in Vegas stays in Vegas," the world teaches us. The true saying, however, is this: what is spoken in confidence should remain in confidence. What is said in the confines of your discussions with your partner stays there unless you have been given permission to share it with others or unless somebody's life is in danger.

Model: Enduring hardships is part of being a good spiritual mentor. As the disciple sees a spiritual mentor deal with struggles, the evidence of the mentor's faith and character shines through. The apostle Paul explained it this way:

And the things that you have heard from me among many witnesses, commit these to faithful men who will be able to teach others also. You therefore must endure hardship as a good soldier of Jesus Christ. No one engaged in warfare entangles himself with the affairs of this life, that he may please him who enlisted him as a soldier. And also if anyone competes in athletics, he is not crowned unless he competes according to the rules. The hardworking farmer must be first to partake of the crops. Consider what I say, and may the Lord give you understanding in all things. (2 Tim. 2:2–7)

Notice that Paul did not say, "If you should have to endure hardship." On the contrary, he warned us that we *must* endure hardship if we are to be good soldiers of Christ. If we are open and honest with our discipleship partner, we will not put on any pretense when times of hardship enter our lives. Enduring such hardship in a godly manner, however, can become the strongest form of modeling a Christ-filled life that anyone can witness.

GOD GAVE US TWO EARS

Developing good listening skills is important to the discipling process. Listening, however, does not mean solving. For most men, solving problems is second nature. Due to God's unique design for men and their personalities, men are usually good at analyzing a situation, coming up with a solution, and implementing that answer. However, in today's world, men are often called upon to use their ears and their mouths with equal ease. Here are a few tips on how to be an outstanding listener.

✳ Look the speaker in the eyes and nod on occasion. Responding with appropriate facial expressions and gestures helps you to stay in touch with the speaker's emotions, not just his words.

✴ Resist the temptation to interrupt constantly. When you interrupt, you are not learning anything; you are merely hindering the other person from speaking. Listen with patience.

✴ Ask good questions that cannot be answered yes or no. But ask questions to help you understand better, not merely to make him think you're interested.

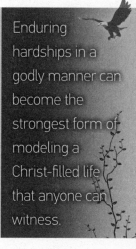

Enduring hardships in a godly manner can become the strongest form of modeling a Christ-filled life that anyone can witness.

✴ Condense and repeat some ideas of the speaker, putting what he has said into your own words. This forces you to really listen to his meaning, not just his words.

✴ Do not immediately give your experiences that are similar to the speaker's; this makes the speaker feel as though you want to be the focus, not that you want to help. You can give your experiences later, but be sure there is a lesson there and that you are not just sharing information.

✴ People love two things in a conversation: the sound of their name and the sound of their voice. As a listener you are responsible to get both of those things to happen, addressing the other person by name, but also allowing the other person to speak freely and without interruption.

✴ Permit the other person to ramble a bit, straying from the central point. Men are hard-wired to "cut to the chase" or "get to the bottom line." When people share a problem, they need to know they are more important than your next appointment. This is especially true with women.

* Ask the speaker, "How can I help?" or, "What do you most need right now?" If you can do whatever it is that he needs, then discuss how best to get that done. If you cannot do what he needs at this time, assure the speaker that you will see what resources you can find that will help meet the need (physical, emotional, financial, spiritual).

* Pray with the speaker and let him know that you will continue to pray about the situation. Then be sure that you do so.

* Check back with the person later in the week to see what else has transpired, whether there have been answers to prayer, whether things have been resolved. Remember that you are a servant in this situation.

Now in order to accomplish this, you must be a man of integrity and loyalty and honesty. Most disciplers agree that a person must be working on being healthy himself in order to help others. And that means you need to be able to keep a person's secrets and that you must be accountable to someone else—someone who is mentoring you.

You also need to be involved at some level in a local church. The Lord's church of today is under attack. Some would say it is not meeting the needs of the people. Others believe that the church has become so "seeker sensitive" that it no longer preaches the gospel, but a watered-down version of Christianity. And there are those who believe that the church of Jesus Christ has gone from "changing lives for Christ" to "just entertaining the troops." Whatever our viewpoint, it is important to remember that the assembling of believers is paramount to spiritual growth and understanding God's Word (Heb. 10:25). Much like the church in Acts, we need to focus on discipling others.

Pastor Jim Putman stated it best:

> Biblically, discipleship is a non-negotiable part of Christ's mission. In Christ's teaching, as well as through the epistles, we are consistently instructed to proclaim, baptize, and teach—all toward the end of making lifelong, die-hard disciples of Jesus Christ who obey His commands. This type of discipleship needs to become the filter for everything we do in church. We want people to say, 'It's my mission to make disciples,' rather than, 'Our church's mission is . . . .' It's that idea of 'This is who I am; it's what I believe in.' And that happens through relationship. You can't give someone else what you haven't owned.[6]

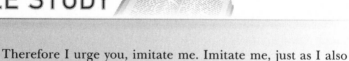

BIBLE STUDY

> Therefore I urge you, imitate me. Imitate me, just as I also imitate Christ. (1 Cor. 4:16; 11:1)

☐ Why did Paul urge his readers to imitate him? Why is imitation a vital part of discipling and being discipled?

☐ Whom do you tend to imitate? When have you consciously decided that you wanted to imitate a particular person in responding to some situation? How did it change your reaction to that situation?

☐ Review the section "God Gave Us Two Ears." How good a listener are you? What areas do you need to strengthen?

MISSION
SUPREME

> Unless God's people have a clear
> understanding of where they are
> headed, the probability of a successful
> journey is severely limited. Unless you
> attend to His call upon your life and
> ministry, you are likely to experience
> confusion, weariness, dissipation, and
> impotence.
> —**George Barna,** *The Power of Vision*[1]

For many years I was utilized as a demonstrator, trainer, television personality, and speaker for the fishing tackle industry. As a Hall of Fame fisherman and former professional bass fisherman, I had the privilege of developing abundant knowledge and skills on a variety of equipment. I definitely had the fishing fever and utilized every opportunity to fish places most people can only dream about.

It was during one of my filming trips to New Zealand that my fishing challenge of a lifetime occurred. Thanks to the generosity of a number of sponsors, I assembled an assortment of tackle that could be used to slay a variety of species while in this pristine paradise. Unfortunately, the skipper of the boat did not think my gear was heavy enough to challenge the big marlin found off the east coast of the North Island, so we quickly stowed my gear in the galley. After convincing him that we needed to have at least one rod on display for the sponsor, he reluctantly placed my rod out with the shortest line to the stern of the boat.

When Jesus talked about discipleship, He told His disciples that if they followed Him He would make them into something new: a new creation, a true disciple.

I am a proactive fisherman and love casting too much to ever consider being a full-time deep-water fisherman. Trolling gets old for me after an hour. The annoying hum of the diesel engines spraying their stinky exhaust into the otherwise pure air, along with the rocking of the boat, is not my idea of fun. But along with all the stream and lake fishing we filmed, the video producers seemed to think we needed some footage of me trying to catch a marlin.

After ten hours of trolling and no fish on board, and with only a few minutes to go before we headed back to shore, a huge marlin appeared about two hundred yards behind the boat. The striped marlin began chasing the outriggers (lures on a line) about seventy-five yards behind the boat. After playing around with four of the five lures on the water, the marlin made a drive to the back of the boat and savagely attacked my little lure—held in place by thirty-pound monofilament line on a rod designed to catch fish up to forty pounds.

When the 265-pound marlin grabbed the lure, I knew the battle was on. I grabbed the rod and set the hook. The stand-up fighting gear I was using created even more of a challenge in breaking the spirit of this hard-fighting fish. After what seemed

Jesus came to earth to give us a new
heart and to change us from the inside out.

like two years (according to the captain, it was about thirty minutes), the beautiful multicolored marlin came up close to the
boat. We took video footage from both above and underwater
as the big bruiser was tagged and then set free. He disappeared
about one hundred feet down into the deep blue Pacific Ocean.

I occasionally still provide seminars at various sports shows.
Usually during the question and answer period, someone in the
audience will ask me what has been my most memorable fishing
challenge. I usually tell them the marlin story. But when it comes
to the Ultimate Fishing Challenge, I share with them the words
of Christ: "Follow Me, and I will make you fishers of men" (Matt.
4:19).

We have discussed what it means to be a disciple and spiritual mentor. We have gained an understanding that discipleship
is a relational process. When Jesus talked about discipleship, He
told His disciples that if they followed Him He would make them
into something new: a new creation, a true disciple. This suggests
that Jesus had to "un-make" certain attitudes, motivations, and
behaviors of these men. To do the re-making, He would need
His followers to yield their lives and obey His commands.

Jesus came to earth to give us a new heart and to change us
from the inside out. Rather than just obey the laws written in
stone, He asks us to search our souls for how God imprints His
love and laws on our hearts. His ways are often contrary to our
worldly ideas. He also asks us to love the unlovely, to pray for our

enemies, to not judge others unless we want to be judged, and to turn away from temptations.

Often men are willing to yield their lives to a mission or goal bigger than themselves. Many of our brave Medal of Honor recipients were people who gave everything to save others because their vision was beyond their own lives. In the same way, men can become committed disciple-makers when they are challenged to view the discipleship process as a mission field within the context of their friendships, experience, jobs, hobbies, and passions. Many men will follow a dedicated leader who has a vision for seeing Christianity as a team sport. An example of this is a famous saying attributed to Vince Lombardi, the legendary coach of the Green Bay Packers: "If you play a man's game, men come to play."

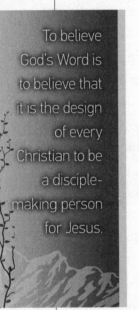

To believe God's Word is to believe that it is the design of every Christian to be a disciple-making person for Jesus.

There is value to the corporate body utilizing its many gifts and talents to connect with others. Jesus Himself had twelve major followers. He had a team. As in the time of Christ, we need a team that is dedicated to the mission of advancing the Word of God to those who do not know Christ. For those who suggest, "I can live the Christian life alone," I would point them to read Scripture; Christ has challenged us to go unto all the nations and tribes of the world (Matt. 28:19; Mark 16:15).

Each one of us is responsible to share the good news with those God brings into our path; however, we need each other to fulfill Christ's command and Great Commission. We were never intended to do the Christian experience on our own, living a "lone ranger" type of lifestyle. The pastors, elders, men's leaders, and Bible teachers are in the church to help equip the members to make disciples. Most unsaved people won't attend church or go to a crusade, but they do know Christians who participate in these events. Thus, sharing the gospel with the unsaved is where each of us needs to become involved. It is in the marketplace of life that each of us sees hurting and lost people that the church doesn't even know about.

As of 2012, there are 195 nations in the world.[2] Rick Warren has stated that there are around five thousand identifiable tribes in the world.[3] Warren's church has taken the Great Commission literally and has embarked upon sending disciples from his church to all the nations and tribes of the earth. What a great vision! How about you? Are you willing to cross the street and meet with a neighbor who might be struggling with a divorce or the death of a loved one or the loss of a job?

INTENTIONAL SPIRITUAL MENTORS

To believe God's Word is to believe that it is the design of every Christian to be a disciple-making person for Jesus. It is the responsibility of every church to equip, motivate, and deploy its members to serve our Lord. As Jesus was an intentional leader, so every pastor, elder, men's leader, dad, mom, small group leader, and friend of an unsaved person is also a person of influence. Thus, we all have the responsibility of being an intentional spiritual mentor. We lead by example, discipline, and seeking to apply the Word of God in our daily living. Intentional disciples buy into the process of developing disciples using Christ's modeling and value a team approach (the church) to reaching others.

An intentional disciple knows the spirit and gifting of those he works with (Eph. 4:11–13). Some readers will say, "I'm not educated and trained as an intentional spiritual mentor." Spiritual Mentors are men who come from all walks of life. They are men who have an interest to see others come to Christ and grow in their faith. Being intentional about our approach to the process will require preparation on our part.

We can't model what we don't know; hence a good understanding of God's Word is important to our ability to be transparent, supportive, and real to those we meet. We strive to obtain a biblical worldview in order to teach others the same. Spiritual mentors are guided by the Holy Spirit to understand where a person is in his spiritual journey. Are the people God has put in your path dead to spiritual things, new in the faith, young in their understanding of God's Word, or seeking to dig deeper into knowing God and making Him known?

RELATIONAL PROCESS

In the last chapter I explained the importance of using a relational process that attracts and will interest people to grow in their faith. As Jesus demonstrated, before He asked His followers to have faith in Him, He welcomed them into a "come and see" period (John 1). Building a solid relationship is one of the most important aspects to men coming to faith.

While there is a purpose and plan for listening to a forty-minute message on a Sunday morning, the most effective way to reach an unsaved person is for each of us to become a friend to that person. Making disciples is not simply transferring information in a well-prepared sermon or devotional. It is more about walking with a struggling and lost individual through his problems and challenges. Large group settings have their place but are very intimidating to the person initially seeking to walk with the Lord. Small group environments or one-on-one experiences in a real-life setting (golfing, fishing, barbecuing, watching a movie or sports together) are environments where your modeling of Christ's love and care can be expressed. With all Christ did in presenting messages to assembled crowds, most of His time was spent in a small group setting with the twelve men He chose to follow Him. Relationship makes the message real.

> We all have the responsibility of being an intentional spiritual mentor.

When we look at the book of Acts, we see that the early church met in homes, in courtyards, and around the tasks they had within the villages. These people weren't perfect and were busy with all the duties and responsibilities of life (job, kids, upkeep of a home, etc.). Despite their busy schedules, imperfections, disagreements, and varied backgrounds, they came together for the purpose of growing our Lord's church. They knew that being together was better than trying to grow their faith alone.

The apostle Paul recognized the importance of relationships and unity in the body when he wrote these words:

> As a prisoner of the Lord, I urge you: Live a life that is worthy of the calling He has *graciously* extended to you. Be humble. Be gentle. Be patient. Tolerate one another in *an atmosphere thick with* love. Make every effort to preserve the unity the Spirit has already created, with peace binding you together. There is one body and one Spirit, just as you were all called to pursue one hope. There is one Lord *Jesus,* one *living* faith, one ceremonial washing through baptism, and one God—the

Father over all who is above all, through all, and in all (Eph. 4:1–6 The Voice).

Jesus reminded us that we will be accepted by others as disciples first for our love (John 13:34–35). He didn't say others will come to faith by our great intellectual capabilities about our faith, or the laws we obey, or the miracles He does through us, or because we are wealthy, healthy, or wise. Christ told us that it is our love, our relationships with others, that best testifies about our faith.

I recall a time when I saw a group of homeless men from the shelter who came to one of our Men's Ministry Catalyst events. They were standing together in the lobby before the program, and their lack of proper dress and obvious personal hygiene problems was a put-off to some of our greeters. I decided to greet them with the love of Jesus by giving each guy a warm handshake and a manly hug. One of the guys said, "Pastor, you don't want to hug me— I'm dirty and I stink." I said, "It doesn't matter to me. A missionary from Africa taught us that hugging someone means I'm wearing their presence for the rest of the day." I greeted him with an extra-big hug. The rest of the day, his body odor and smoke-saturated clothing smell lingered upon my clothing. Though it was bothersome, it reminded me how Christ loved the unlovely and how He has taught us to do the same. I thought about the fact that our sin-filled lives must have the same stench to a Holy God, but He regularly surrounds us with His love.

> If we were more committed to working through our difficult Christian marriages and personal relationships, then we would have more forgiveness, growth, love, and kindness modeled to our unsaved world.

In today's stress-filled, judgmental world, it is easy to get a critical spirit about a lot of things, including our church or other believers. Paul tells us that the fruit of the Spirit is love, joy, peace, longsuffering, kindness, goodness, faithfulness, gentleness, and self-control (Gal. 5:22–23). How much do these traits manifest themselves in our lives and within our relationships with others, within our church, within our homes, and within our nation? I'm convicted that I need to continue to work on having my relationships right as I also continue to testify of God's faithfulness to me and teach others the gospel of Jesus Christ.

When the process we use to connect with others and build our churches is right, then we will be effective models of Christ. When churches start to care more about building big people in the Lord instead of trying to build big buildings to be filled with uncommitted individuals, we will begin to see real growth in the church.

Don't wait until you have it all together. None of us will ever have it all together. A non-believer watching you in the process of building stronger relationships within your believing community will see firsthand how Christians solve problems. If we were more committed to working through our difficult Christian marriages and personal relationships, then we would have more forgiveness, growth, love, and kindness modeled to our unsaved world.

A relational process and environment includes people who are willing to guide, teach, direct, assist, serve, model, and be transparent and accountable with others. It is a process that evokes trust and respect, thus helping to eliminate fear and suspicion. The process and the environment utilize the gifts of many to help build the faith of a few. Once again, Paul reminds us of something we can bring into our relationship building: "Therefore, as we have opportunity, let us do good to all, especially to those who are of the household of faith" (Gal. 6:10).

REPRODUCIBLE MODEL

Jesus shared with, connected with, and trained those who followed Him in ministry, and He released His disciples to make disciples.[4] Christ intended that the method and model He used to make disciples would be something that was reproducible in every disciple who followed the original twelve. The design for discipleship that Christ modeled was as follows:

1. **Build** bridges to connect with our culture.

2. **Share** the Word of God in practical ways.

3. **Care for and minister** to people right where they are.

4. **Develop** true disciples who can disciple others.

5. **Support** disciple-makers with prayer, resources, and encouragement.

1. BUILD BRIDGES TO CONNECT WITH OUR CULTURE.

English Christian leader Reverend John Stott developed the metaphor of bridge building to our culture:

> If we are to build bridges into the real world, and seek to relate the Word of God to the major themes of life and the major issues of the day, then we have to take seriously both

the biblical text and the contemporary scene. We cannot afford to remain on either side of the cultural divide . . . it is our responsibility to explore the territories on both sides of the ravine until we become thoroughly familiar with them. Only then shall we discern the connections between them and be able to speak the divine Word to the human situation with any degree of sensitivity and accuracy.[5]

As an example of reaching out to others, Jesus took the disciples on a detour just so that He could meet the Samaritan woman at the well in Samaria (John 4). Christ first befriended her and spoke to her in terms that she would understand. Only after He showed compassion and understanding did He then talk to her about the "living water."

We are called to be in the world but not of the world (John 15:19). What have you done lately to reach your community for Christ?

2. SHARE THE WORD OF GOD IN PRACTICAL WAYS.

God wants us to use our gifts, talents, experiences, connections, and opportunities to meet people and share His Word. There are different gifts and ways to present God's Word to others. Peter's approach as seen in Acts 2 was to be direct with people. The apostle Paul was an intellectual person with a gift in exhortation and knowledge. He manifested his abilities in Acts 17 as he addressed the people of Athens. Matthew used an interpersonal and people-centered model to approach others, as seen in Luke 5. Through his friendship with other tax collectors, he invited them to meet Christ. Dorcas was a widow who served Christ and His disciples. In Acts 9 we see her servant's heart and her acts of service as she used her talents to model Christ's love. The blind beggar whom Christ healed went about his disciple-making career with a message of simple faith (Luke 18:35–43). On another occasion, when Jesus again healed a man blind from birth, others tried to test him about the type of miracle that occurred, asking if Jesus was the Messiah. The lonely beggar said in a faithful way, "One thing I know: that though I was blind, now I see" (John 9:25).

Have you ever taken a test to find out what your spiritual gifts are? If you know what your gifts are, how are you using them to connect with the lost?

3. CARE AND MINISTER TO PEOPLE RIGHT WHERE THEY ARE.

Time and time again, Jesus did not ask people to come to His place of comfort or to His synagogue; He went to them. He met the fisherman along the shoreline at the Sea of Galilee. He went out of His way to meet the Samaritan woman at the well. You would find Jesus inside the city gates meeting the blind, paralyzed, and lepers. By title and position you would think that people should have come to Him. As the Prince of Peace, Son of God, and King of all kings, He deserved to be served—yet He chose to serve. He elected to meet people where they felt most at ease and open to accept what Christ taught them.

Are you endeavoring to connect with someone God has put in your path? Are you willing to take the time to go to their work, favorite coffee shop, or home, or to participate in the recreational areas of interest they have?

4. DEVELOP TRUE DISCIPLES WHO CAN DISCIPLE OTHERS.

While thousands heard Peter speak at Pentecost, the disciples knew that they needed to connect with those who accepted Jesus in a more intimate setting. The disciples connected with the new believers at a deeper level where they were able to teach, train, and model the good news through meeting daily in houses and in the temple courtyards where they fellowshipped with a purpose (Acts 2).

The disciples were devoted to the process and the fellowship necessary to help the new converts become spiritual mentors. The new believers had to look at their lives through the lens of Christ's eyes rather than the worldview they held. As Paul preached in Romans 12 and 1 Corinthians 12, each believer has a purpose and should be part of a team to develop a comprehensive process that introduces people to the life-changing ways of Christ. In 1 Corinthians 12 Paul uses the analogy of the human body, teaching us that every Christian is a part of the body of Christ. But a person's body works most effectively when all parts are involved in working together to accomplish one goal. You can't wash the dishes in the kitchen sink if your feet are trying to walk into the next room; in the same way, the individual Christian is most effective when he is working in unity with other members of Christ's body.

Are you trying to go it alone? Wouldn't it be great to connect with other Christians who desire to make a real difference in this

> Each believer has a purpose and should be part of a team to develop a comprehensive process that introduces people to the life-changing ways of Christ.

world by reaching others for Christ? How can you become better connected with other believers in this way?

5. SUPPORT DISCIPLE-MAKERS WITH PRAYER, RESOURCES, AND ENCOURAGEMENT.

In order for us to be successful in developing *intentional spiritual mentors* in a relational process using a reproducible model, we need the prayers, resources, and encouragement of others. When we see the roles Mary and Martha played in supporting and providing for the original twelve, we realize that disciple-making requires a team. In Luke 10:38–42 we see how the exhausted disciples were served by these women, who helped refresh them for the calling God had put on their shoulders.

I believe the church body has a responsibility not just to equip, train, and teach people about discipleship, but also to be encouragers and resource providers to help spiritual mentors do their job. Too often a church forgets about those on the spiritual battlefields because they're so focused on preaching, teaching, and training. We need to remind ourselves to check in with those in the trenches so that they do not become weary or downhearted. Discouragement is the enemy of the soul. Sunday messages alone may not help those who are under spiritual attack. This is why the early church fellowshipped often and assisted the men who were in spiritual battles.

What needs do you have to become a more effective intentional spiritual mentor? Have you shared your desires with others? What kind of team could you put together to help support you in your efforts?

BIBLE STUDY

Read 1 Corinthians 12:12–27.

☐ Why does Paul use the analogy of the human body to describe the relationship that Christians have with one another? What important principle does this illustrate concerning Christian fellowship?

☐ What does Paul mean when he says that "there should be no schism in the body" (v. 25)? What sort of "schisms" can occur within the Christian church? What results when they happen?

☐ Give practical examples of what different body parts can do for the work of Christ. For example, the hands might perform acts of service for others; the ears be skilled listeners and empathizers; the tongue gifted in preaching the Word of God. What body part best describes the roles that you play in God's work?

MAKING AN **ENVIRONMENT** TO GROW MEN

> But you are a chosen generation, a royal priesthood, a holy nation, His own special people, that you may proclaim the praises of Him who called you out of darkness into His marvelous light.
> **—1 Peter 2:9**

My parents came from dysfunctional families. Adding to the confusion about their perspective on good parenting were their different religious backgrounds. Mom was brought up in a predominantly Mormon home, and Dad was reared in the Catholic tradition. He was an altar boy at one time. After they were married, their choice of denominations became Methodism.

I can remember sitting in church with my folks on Sunday morning thinking the last thing in the world I would ever want to be was a preacher. It was not until I was in my teens that a good friend presented Christ to me. Neither of my parents was very deep into their faith, so I looked for a mentor who could help me understand what it really meant to be a follower of Jesus.

Author James Houston once said, "Perhaps coming from broken homes, or broken marriages, or other experiences of dysfunctional relationships, people are looking to mentors to make a difference in their lives."[1]

When I graduated high school, I was very young in the Lord and lacked any good pre-college counseling, so I ended up in a very liberal secular college. In a college of seventeen thousand students, there were only two pre-theology students—and we had an atheist philosophy professor as our advisor. The liberal professors had their way with me, and soon I bought into their viewpoint on many theological issues. Upon graduation I had the opportunity to work for a large two-county park system and was placed under a man who would eventually change my life.

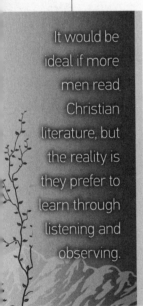

It would be ideal if more men read Christian literature, but the reality is they prefer to learn through listening and observing.

Stan Smith seemed like a common name, yet this man was anything but common. As a spirit-filled Christian who was bright and experienced, he freely shared his compassion and deep love for Jesus. He understood the biblical model of discipleship and embraced God's Word. His biblical worldview was contrary to my self-derived hypocritical approach to theology. I was lost amid the vain worldly philosophies of life, living, and manhood.

As I espoused my thoughts about God and Christ, Stan would patiently bring me back to what the Bible taught. He would remind me of the words found in Proverbs: "There is a way that seems right to a man, but its end is the way of death" (14:12). Stan quickly won my trust and became my best friend and spiritual mentor—a "godfather." He was the same age as my dad, but Stan was equipped and willing

God made most men to understand comprehensive thoughts through visualization, example, and story.

to discuss deep theological issues that concerned my spiritual well-being. He allowed God to work through him, as he helped me work on a number of personal problems connected to my distorted theological perspective.

Stan didn't judge me or become critical about my initial inability to accept and apply the Word of God that marked his life. As a World War II survivor, he had been through many ordeals that helped shape his personality and view of God. He saw men struggle with issues of faith and didn't give up on them. He wasn't going to give up on me.

There were two major things that Stan modeled for me that I attempt to utilize in my discipling of others: he used story and examples to implant God's Word; and he would always make time to reach down to the younger generations and teach them about God. Stan knew that when he began to speak through stories I listened and absorbed. The biblical principles he wove into the stories helped me see that God's Word was real and could be applied to my daily struggles. Stan made a good mentor because he was real, honest, and rich in the life experiences necessary to be a mentor. It is difficult for a twentysomething pastor or men's leader to become a mentor of men when he really hasn't experienced much of life. It's for that reason that the patriarchs of our churches are so valuable.

Stan helped me see that my priorities of trying to be important rather than do what's important was not God's plan for being a man of significance. He coached me so that I could value the time with my young family and recognize its importance. As a young man Stan had spent too much time at work and not enough time raising his three kids. I could feel the pain and sorrow of his regrets and failures. He was transparent and loving in how he inspired me to see beyond the American dream of fame, power, and fortune so that I would not make the same mistakes he did.

ORALITY

As much as we wish men would read, listen, and communicate on spiritual and personal matters, most men feel uncomfortable baring their souls on spiritual issues with other men or even their spouses. Most Christian bookstore managers would tell us that 80 percent of the books purchased will be by women—including books written expressly for men. Oftentimes I will be surveying literature in a Christian bookstore and be the only male in the store. It would be ideal if more men read Christian literature, but the reality is they prefer to learn through listening and observing.

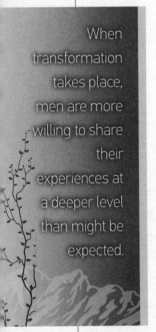

When transformation takes place, men are more willing to share their experiences at a deeper level than might be expected.

Today there are many great Bible teachers. Those who have most influenced my life utilize story as a way to connect with their audiences. People like Chuck Swindoll, David Jeremiah, Charles Stanley, Chip Ingram, Rick Warren, Jim Putman, and Robert Lewis have a way of telling stories, anecdotes, parables, and allegories that directly connect men to the Word of God. This approach is sometimes called *orality*, the art of sharing through story. Orality utilizes stories to share information that leads a person to a new understanding of truth. Certainly this is a method that Jesus used on numerous occasions to connect with His audience and teach them eternal truths.

God made most men to understand comprehensive thoughts through visualization, example, and story. Men tend to be more left-brain oriented and gravitate toward logic, reasoning, rational thinking, and problem solving. Our ministry, Men's Ministry Catalyst, has developed some of the most comprehensive curricula and advanced resources on men's ministry in the country. These tools and resources have helped men in the disciple-making area. One reason they have connected well with men is that we use storytelling to approach various topics.

A BRIDGE TO THE UNSAVED

I had the opportunity to excel in fishing and hunting. As a Hall of Fame fisherman and record-book archer, I've been around the world on various fishing and hunting excursions. Over thirty-three years ago, through the encouragement of another of my mentors, I utilized my passion for the outdoors as a bridge to connect with men. I remember during one trip when several things had gone wrong and we were trying to keep warm so we wouldn't freeze to death, I had an opportunity to share with my companion the faithfulness and protection God provides to those He loves. Our conversation over that campfire changed the heart of this man toward things of the Lord. Knowing that there were over sixty million fishermen and almost thirteen million hunters over the age of sixteen, and figuring that over half of these populations are male, there is no shortage of unsaved guys to communicate God's truth through outdoor adventure stories. People have a way of remembering something if it's in the context of a good adventure story. I think Jesus knew this and often hid transforming truths within His stories (Matt. 13:11–13) that not only impacted His twelve disciples but have resonated with followers for over two thousand years.

I'm always amazed how I can remember details of those things that interest me. Batting averages of key baseball players, quarterback ratings, and the speed of the latest Corvette are easy things for me to remember because they connect with information that have stories behind the statistics. The apostle Paul stated that we need to renew our minds with God's Word so as not to be *con*formed to the world around us; instead, we are to be *trans*formed by His Word and Spirit (Rom. 12:1–2).

Often men see themselves as independent self-starters, and maybe even a little bit prideful or hard-hearted. Storytelling has a way of breaking through barriers and softening hearts so they can hear and feel emotion. When transformation takes place, men are more willing to share their experiences at a deeper level than might be expected.

WHY IS STORY IMPORTANT?

As previously mentioned, the primary way Jesus taught was through the use of storytelling, or orality: "Jesus gave all these teachings to the crowd in parables. Indeed, He spoke only in parables in fulfillment of the prophetic words *of the psalms*: 'I will open My mouth in parables; I will tell them things that have been hidden and obscure since the very beginning of the world'" (Matt. 13:34–35 The Voice).

Whether answering the profound or trick questions from the priests, Sadducees, and Pharisees, or talking to the common man, Christ most often used stories (Matt. 18:21–35; Luke 10:30–37). His stories provided questions and conviction that resulted in having people rethink Scripture at a deeper level or end up condemning themselves because of the lessons being taught through Christ's spoken word. His message came through stronger than would normally occur by general lecturing. His words shaped ideas and created interest among the people to ask further questions. Life lessons were hammered out over the anvil of modeled truth.

I often use storytelling when chatting with passengers next to me on a plane. Most often I will be diligently typing on my laptop, which usually brings a question from the person next to me about what I'm working on. I usually respond with, "I'm working on a book." They then have to ask, "What kind of book?" I reply, "Hopefully, something that will change the hearts of men." My short but open-ended responses cause the inquisitive person to come back with more questions until we finally get around to talking about why men are in trouble; how a belief in God can help change their motives, hearts, actions, and direction; and then how that will affect our country.

> Orality is especially effective in discipling or speaking to a group of young Christians. It is putting God's teachings into an understandable form so that people can be encouraged to grow deeper in their faith.

Storytelling or even humor can also be used to open up conversations that lead to God's Word. If I sense that the passenger next to me is nervous about flying, I will ask specific questions that lead to a dialogue like this:

Jim to passenger: Do you fly much?

Nervous passenger: No, not really. I don't like flying.

Jim: You know, I don't like flying either because of two primary concerns.

Nervous passenger: What are your concerns?

Jim: The first one is, when it's my time to go I have no problem with dying, but if it's the pilot's time to go then we all go with him. Secondly, Jesus said, "Lo, I'm with you always."

Follow-up comment from Jim: You know, worry used to captivate too much of my time, but I found a secret to help eliminate worry.

Inquisitive passenger: What secret did you find?

Jim: I found the comforting words that God gave us through Scripture, and the power and presence of the Holy Spirit allows me to trust Him. I had to learn about letting God be in control. Can I share with you some thoughts that might help you?

Do you remember being a kid and someone would say, "Would you like to hear a good story?" Most of us would say, "Sure." Sometimes the story would start off with, "Once upon a time," and usually we would lean forward in our chairs to hear what followed. Orality is especially effective in discipling or speaking to a group of young Christians. It is putting God's teachings into an understandable form so that people can be encouraged to grow deeper in their faith.

Once a person is a mature Christian, I don't normally use storytelling as the primary way to communicate with him. The mature audience is ready for discovery at a deeper level; hence I will still use short anecdotes and parables from my life or something I observed to set up the reading and preaching of God's Word.

There are powerful stories throughout Scripture that men will listen to if presented in the proper way. It is not unspiritual to paraphrase a Bible story in your language while providing real-life examples that connect the audience to the thoughts presented in the literal words found in Scripture. If you can capture a man's attention with a Bible story, you can direct him back to reading the actual verses that will transform his life. Storytelling is not the same as reading a verse-by-verse account. Once again, Real Life Ministries has some demonstrations you can download from their website, www.reallifeministries.com.

Orality allows a person delivering the message to be a little more relaxed and approachable. The idea is to get people into the Word, asking questions, verifying what they heard, and digging deeper for truth. An intentional leader will listen carefully to the responses of the individual or small group members so he can pick up on where they are spiritually. Then he can prepare future lessons to address their specific needs. The other advantage to a storytelling approach is that men who previously sat on the bench (uninvolved Christians) see that it doesn't take a Doctor of Divinity degree to become a spiritual mentor. Spectators become participants when they realize that, if they can tell a story and be transparent, they can teach and reach others.

At the end of the day we see that God uses our faith, talents, gifts, personalities, and experiences to form our character. And it is within our character that people will experience the modeling of Christ. The world-famous author and traveler Rudyard Kipling gave us this poem as a reminder that character counts.

IF

If you can keep your head when all about you
Are losing theirs and blaming it on you;
If you can trust yourself when all men doubt you,
But make allowance for their doubting too:
If you can wait and not be tired by waiting,
Or, being lied about, don't deal in lies,
Or being hated don't give way to hating,
And yet don't look too good, nor talk too wise;
If you can dream—and not make dreams your master;
If you can think—and not make thoughts your aim,
If you can meet with Triumph and Disaster
And treat those two impostors just the same:
If you can bear to hear the truth you've spoken
Twisted by knaves to make a trap for fools,
Or watch the things you gave your life to, broken,
And stoop and build'em up with worn-out tools;
If you can make one heap of all your winnings
And risk it on one turn of pitch-and-toss,
And lose, and start again at your beginnings,
And never breathe a word about your loss:
If you can force your heart and nerve and sinew
To serve your turn long after they are gone,
And so hold on when there is nothing in you
Except the Will which says to them: "Hold on!"

If you can talk with crowds and keep your virtue,
Or walk with Kings—nor lose the common touch,
If neither foes nor loving friends can hurt you,
If all men count with you, but none too much:
If you can fill the unforgiving minute
With sixty seconds' worth of distance run,
Yours is the Earth and everything that's in it,
And—which is more—you'll be a Man, my son![4]

BIBLE STUDY

Read Matthew 18:21–35.

☐ What is the central message of Jesus' story here, in your own words? Why did He tell this story rather than simply stating His principles on forgiveness?

☐ How much money did the servant owe the king (v. 24)? How much did the fellow servant owe the servant (v. 28)? Why did Jesus include these details? What was He suggesting to His audience?

☐ In what ways is a story or parable a more effective way of teaching than a more didactic, fact-based approach? What might be some possible drawbacks to the storytelling approach?

MISSION
POSSIBLE

And Jesus came and spoke to them, saying, "All authority has been given to Me in heaven and on earth. Go therefore and make disciples of all the nations, baptizing them in the name of the Father and of the Son and of the Holy Spirit, teaching them to observe all things that I have commanded you; and lo, I am with you always, even to the end of the age."

—Matthew 28:18–20

ANDREW: THE ULTIMATE DISCIPLE (FISHER OF MEN)

Andrew was an ordinary man, an uneducated laborer who earned a living by catching fish. But there was one thing that made Andrew unique: he was one of the first men to drop what he was doing and follow Jesus (John 1:35–39).

We can picture Andrew as a man whose longings and aspirations went far beyond the daily grind of being a fisherman. He had a deep longing to understand eternal truth, and he would spend his days gazing over the gunwale of his boat, hoping that someday he might see someone who could direct him to God. He, like so many other Jewish individuals, eagerly awaited the fulfillment of the promise of the Messiah.

The smelly business of supplying fish to the homes of Capernaum was no easy task. He would be working throughout the night on capricious Lake Galilee, laboring long and hard to cast his nets and haul in fish. As daylight approached, he had to deliver the fish to Capernaum, catch a few hours of sleep, then mend his nets and ready the boat for more fishing. The nets had to be properly balanced to throw and would require adjustment on a daily basis. The time and location of the fishing activity had to be carefully planned; the fishermen did not randomly row into the middle of the lake and toss out their nets. And fishing with nets required others to help pull the nets, clean the fish, and prepare them for the village.

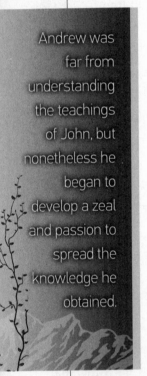

Andrew was far from understanding the teachings of John, but nonetheless he began to develop a zeal and passion to spread the knowledge he obtained.

And somehow during his hectic day, Andrew also made time to walk miles to the Jordan River to meet a man known as John the Baptist and to listen to him teach about another person who was coming: someone called the Light of the World. Andrew was far from understanding the teachings of John, but nonetheless he began to develop a zeal and passion to spread the knowledge he obtained. Whatever he learned, he enthusiastically went out and shared it with others.

Then one day Andrew and John the Baptist were talking together when John suddenly broke off. "Behold," he cried out,

Disciples like Andrew formed the
backbone of the Christian church and continue
to be the salt of the earth.

pointing toward a man walking in their direction, "the Lamb of God!" Without a moment's hesitation, Andrew turned away from John the Baptist and fell into step behind this man named Jesus. Andrew knew almost nothing about Him, but John's testimony was enough; he believed in that moment that this Jesus was the Messiah he'd been looking for (John 1:35–39).

During the early days of following Jesus, Andrew's fishing background helped him grow in his understanding of what is required to become a disciple of Christ, simply because he already knew what was required to become a successful fisherman. He knew the importance of discipline. He recognized the hours of toil and sweat necessary to complete daily tasks. And he knew the value of authority; someone had taught him to fish, and someone had to be in charge when men were fishing. As a young Jewish man, Andrew also learned about the authority of the Word of God and the authority of the leaders in the tabernacle and in the temple in Jerusalem. Their authority was complete and it was to be respected.

Andrew fixed his gaze upon the Lord and began to listen and follow the words of Christ. This budding disciple was continually using his fishing background to meet people in the marketplace of life and share his faith. He began by introducing his brother Peter to Jesus (John 1:40–42), an outgoing and boisterous man whose gifts eventually allowed him to become the leader of the apostolic band. Andrew, by contrast, was the humble crusader, the less-flamboyant brother who was chiefly concerned with spreading the good news of Messiah—yet disciples like Andrew formed the backbone of the Christian church and continue to be the salt of the earth.

Andrew was eager to bring anyone to Christ, even little children. On one occasion he introduced Jesus to a lad who had five loaves and two fish packed for lunch (John 6:8–9). On another occasion we find Andrew doing the work of evangelism by bringing a group of Greek men to Jesus (John 12:20–22). The Greeks had come to Philip with the request to see Jesus, but they were Gentiles who had come to celebrate Passover, and Philip did not know what to do with them. It was Andrew who quickly realized that they must be taken to Jesus. In these ways we discover that Andrew was an early evangelist for the kingdom of God.

PRINCIPLES OF DISCIPLESHIP FROM ANDREW

Sharing his faith came naturally for Andrew because he took what he saw and heard and shared the information in a natural way without feeling guilty that he was not a great prophet, priest, or Pharisee. He also practiced his beliefs, and as he did, it became a natural part of his personality. It is interesting to note that Jesus didn't choose the most educated men of His time or the most religious men of that day, but He sought out common men to be the ones responsible for spreading the gospel. He chose men willing to learn, to grow, and to put themselves under His authority, and they called Him "Rabboni" or "teacher."

Andrew's background as a fisherman enabled him to make a quick transition into being a fisher of men. Andrew learned about Jesus. He carefully watched Him, listened to Him, and attempted to emulate Him in every way in his life. He was also quick to see that Jesus could meet needs that he could not meet by himself. Here are some of the principles of discipleship that we find illustrated in his life.

1. **Andrew sought to be unselfish in representing Christ.** He knew that his brother Peter was a natural, instinctive leader. It didn't bother Andrew to take the back seat.

2. **Andrew was an optimist.** He saw the little boy with the five loaves and two fish as someone who could be used by Jesus.

3. **Andrew was not prejudiced.** At a time when races and cultures did not mix with one another, Andrew sought to share God's Word with all people.

THE FEAR-GUILT CYCLE

Discipling others should feel comfortable and never pressured. One of our responsibilities as Christians is to always be ready to give a witness for the hope that is within us (1 Peter 3:15). Most fishermen I know are excited to share with others about a new lure that is really catching fish. That same joy and comfort should follow as we share with others about the most exciting news anyone could hear: that their sins are forgiven and they can have eternal life. For some, the struggle of sharing our faith comes with the fact that we don't feel equipped or prepared to share our faith.

Andrew didn't allow his position, education, or lack of preparation to stand in the way of telling people about Jesus.

Unfortunately, too many people allow issues to stand in the way of just plainly and simply presenting God's Word. Often a guilt cycle results and eventually leads to fears about sharing one's faith with others.

The cycle works this way: First you feel guilty that you aren't sharing your faith. You don't share your faith because you have a fear of doing it. Or, if you do break through the fear and actually share your faith, you suddenly feel guilty because you didn't do it right.

We need to break that cycle. The cycle is much like a person volunteering to serve in the military. Very few men would serve if they expected to be sent on the front lines of battle without the proper training. A recruit usually completes several tests that determine his area of expertise and then is sent to basic training. After his basic training he receives more advanced training in his area of specialization. Once he completes that assignment, he will usually get some supervised experience in the field so he can better anticipate how he will react under fire. And throughout all of this intensive and extended training, he is under the authority of the teacher.

It should be the same for the believer. He must be equipped with some training, appropriate resources, and an opportunity to utilize his testimony in a controlled environment, and then he can be placed into experiences that fit his gifting and training. It is imperative that he have a teacher—one who is in authority—to guide, instruct, and demonstrate the lessons of life witnessing.

> If we adopt an attitude of prayer throughout the day by asking God for His guidance, then we have an opportunity to really know God's plan for our lives.

PACKING OUR BACKPACKS

Before attempting to go on the spiritual battlefield, a disciple must prepare his spirit and mind for the opportunities God will put before him. We need to pack our lives with three fundamental things before we set out to fight the good fight. The first thing to put in our spiritual packs is to devote ourselves to prayer. That doesn't mean this is all we do, but there must be a pattern of consistent praying that undergirds everything we do. If we adopt an attitude of prayer throughout the day by asking God for His guidance, then we have an opportunity to really know God's plan for our lives. Scripture reminds us to be "continuing steadfastly in prayer" (Rom. 12:12). This was an important habit in the lives of Christians during the early church: "These all continued with one accord in prayer and supplication" (Acts 1:14; 2:42; 6:4). Paul urged his readers to "continue earnestly in prayer, being vigilant in it with thanksgiving" (Col. 4:2).

The second item to include in our spiritual packs is accessing the power of the Holy Spirit. Through prayer, meditation, and reading God's Word, we open our minds and hearts to the filling of the Spirit. We yield and surrender ourselves to be under the influence of the Spirit of God. Instead of doing only what we want to do, we seek to be guided by Him. Instead of approaching our challenges with our own strength and abilities, we are empowered and guided by God's wisdom and strength. This is a mystery of Christianity and one that we believe on faith. Jesus told us that it was necessary for Him to go away but that He would send the Teacher, the Counselor, who would instruct us in all things (John 14:26).

The apostle Paul tells us, "Don't drink wine excessively. The drunken path *is a reckless path. It* leads nowhere. Instead, let God fill you with the Holy Spirit" (Eph. 5:18 The Voice). And again, we see the Christians of the early church submitting themselves to the power of the Holy Spirit: "They finished their prayer, and immediately the whole place where they had gathered began to shake. All the disciples were filled with the Holy Spirit, and they began speaking God's message with courageous confidence" (Acts 4:31 The Voice).

Instead of approaching our challenges with our own strength and abilities, we are empowered and guided by God's wisdom and strength.

The third part of our pack is that of cultivating great faith. But this immediately raises the question, what is faith? The writer of Hebrews defined it for us: "Now faith is the substance of things hoped for, the evidence of things not seen" (11:1). That is, we choose to believe in those things that cannot be concretely proven by our senses or by human reason, choosing instead to believe that those things are true because God is faithful, and what He says is always true.

In a sense, then, the act of faith is like saying "amen" to God: "You said it's true, Lord—so be it!" In his marvelous work *The Confessions*, St. Augustine states, "Faith is to believe what we do not see, and the reward of this faith is to see what we believe."[1] The classic acrostic also captures this essence of faith: Forsaking All I Take Him.

God is always challenging our faith, and in so doing He builds our relationship with Him and helps us grow into intimacy with Him. It's through the hard times that we learn to trust and thank God. Our recognition and need for God amidst our trials and tribulation is key to knowing and trusting Him. Intimacy with God is often molded in the furnace of great despair and discouragement. When we lift up our petitions to the Lord, we should always ask ourselves if they will challenge our faith. Asking God for guidance will help us determine the origin of His voice in our hearts.

When Jesus was on earth, He was always looking for people to respond in faith. Indeed, He could just speak and that would be the end of it, but in many instances His voice required an act of faith on someone's part to comprehend what He had revealed. The same is true with how He works in us today.

LOVE ONE ANOTHER

Too often we get caught up in feeling that we need more education, more study, more teaching, more, more, more. When Jesus washed the disciples' feet, He was giving them a lesson in being the servant of servants. He didn't tell them what to do; He showed them.

> So when He had washed their feet, taken His garments, and sat down again, He said to them, "Do you know what I have done to you? You call Me Teacher and Lord, and you say well, for so I am. If I then, your Lord and Teacher, have washed your feet, you also ought to wash one another's feet. For I have given you an example, that you should do as I have done to you." (John 13:12–15)

Later on in the gospel of John, Jesus told the disciples, "A new commandment I give to you, that you love one another; as I have loved you, that you also love one another" (13:34).

How did Jesus love them? By serving them, teaching them, wanting what was best for each of them, having patience with them, spending time with them, being their authority. In Matthew 4:21–23, the disciples saw Jesus model teaching, preaching, and healing. He demonstrated for them compassion, faith, and love. He taught in order to show them a concern for understanding and communicating with others. He healed to show them a concern for the connection between body, mind, and spirit. He preached to others to show them God's plan for their lives and the importance of immersing ourselves in the Word of God.

When Jesus taught His disciples, it was most often done with stories and not with the law or heavy doses of theology. Rather, He humbly approached teaching in common language with practical ideas of how to live. We normally refer to these stories as *parables*. The parables Jesus taught always had a surface message that was related to the story and a deeper meaning that was related to the lives of everyone listening. The Sermon on the Mount was about principles of life: "Blessed are the poor in spirit, for theirs is the kingdom of heaven. Blessed are those who mourn, for they shall be comforted. Blessed are the meek, for they shall inherit the earth. Blessed are those who hunger and thirst for righteousness, for they shall be filled" (Matt. 5:3–6).

LOVING BY MODELLING

Christ modeled His beliefs. Peter tells us to "grow in the grace and knowledge of our Lord and Savior Jesus Christ" (2 Peter

3:18). Jesus walked with His disciples and demonstrated His faith as they walked together through various challenges and opportunities. Our culture operates at such a hectic pace that we don't take the time to really walk with those in need of spiritual encouragement. In fact, we do not take the time to really walk (and listen) to those closest to us in life: our family. It is the journey through life that allows us to bump into people of every walk and stratum of life where we can share our thoughts and attitudes.

The literal translation of the command found in Matthew 28:19 is, "As you are going, make disciples!" It is in daily experience at work, in school, in the home that we allow people to have windows into our lives so that they can see how we treat others, how we handle conflict, what we do with our spare time, what understandings we bring to challenging opportunities, and how we deal with temptation.

AFRAID TO TAKE RISKS

Teddy Roosevelt once said, "Far better it is to dare mighty things, to win glorious triumphs, even though checkered by failure, than to take rank with those poor spirits who neither enjoy much nor suffer much, because they live in the gray twilight that knows not victory nor defeat."[2] When Andrew the Lord's disciple went fishing, he faced all sorts of dangers. His boat might sink; a storm might come up suddenly and sweep him overboard; at the very least, he might return home empty-handed after a long day of fruitless effort. There were all sorts of bad possibilities that he and his fellow fishermen faced as they pushed off from the shore each morning—but those possibilities did not prevent them from fishing.

A good fisherman has to constantly refine and perfect his skills, while also taking some risks. It takes practice and commitment, learning how to cast more accurately, studying what baits and lures work best in different conditions, and so much more. Great fishermen aren't born; they're made. Success comes from devotion, a great deal of hard work, discipline, and the refinement of great mentors and coaches who help shape and mold men into great fishermen.

So it is with being a disciple. Jesus is perpetually perfecting the saints for the work of ministry. You and I, as disciples, are called to live like Christ and make other disciples who can, in turn, live like Christ and make other disciples. Discipleship is apprenticeship, the process of sharing, encouraging, modeling, teaching, listening, and serving. Living like Christ and leading others comes from devotion to God's mission, time in the Word, and time with God. And it takes practice! Representing Christ doesn't come naturally. If we're not grounded in truth and yielded to our Great Mentor and the Final Authority, our best efforts can be misguided, misunderstood, intercepted, and even used by the enemy.

Speaking truth and leading others to a saving knowledge of Christ can feel risky, but the victory is so sweet! The daily practice of living a Christlike life will help keep us from having our intentions and actions intercepted by the evil one. Thankfully, God's grace cuts through our own inadequacies. All He asks for is a heart that is fully devoted to Him and willing to take the risk.

> Success comes from devotion, a great deal of hard work, discipline, and the refinement of great mentors and coaches who help shape and mold men into great fishermen.

As we unpack some new thinking about discipleship and what it means to be a spiritual mentor, let's pray that God will open our minds and hearts to a deeper walk with Him. Together we will explore the essence of our faith and calling.

BIBLE STUDY

Read Matthew 28:16–20.

Make a list of the specific things that Jesus commanded His disciples to do. Then define each of those items in your own words.

Based upon your list, what specifically does Jesus call His followers to do? How might a mentor carry out these tasks in a discipling relationship?

Why did Jesus precede His commands by saying, "All authority has been given to Me in heaven and on earth" (v. 18)? How does this statement encourage Christ's followers to be willing to take risks?

MODELING
CHRIST

"Discipleship is a process. God's desire is to etch into our lives the imprint of His Son, Jesus. He is responsible for the construction process of making us like Christ. But He needs yielded, available individuals willing to be shaped, molded, and carved by His hands."

—Ken Carpenter, *Spirit of Revival*[1]

Then He said to them, "Follow Me, and I will make you fishers of men."

—Matthew 4:19

In 1997 my wife and I had the opportunity to help lead an international conference on discipleship held in Auckland, New Zealand. My good kiwi friend John Sax utilized his business and faith-based contacts to put together this South Pacific conference. Together we provided an opportunity for more than two hundred church leaders to participate in the revolutionary work of encouraging churches to explore the essence of what Jesus meant by "go make disciples."

Many of the pastors attending the conference were from denominations that held to formal liturgies and pasty doctrines that were devoid of the real-world experiences that lead to true mentoring. During one of my presentations it became quite obvious that every time I mentioned the words *disciple* or *discipleship*, the assembled group would stir in their seats wondering if everyone was on the same page. This produced a very uncomfortable situation for everyone present.

So in order to address the situation head-on, during my presentation I stopped and shocked the distinguished audience by asking each one of them how they would define *disciple* and *discipleship*. I heard as many definitions as there were people in the audience. All of them had parts of a biblical definition, but none completely satisfied what God says about being a disciple or what is meant by discipleship.

In this chapter we will consider a number of possible definitions for a disciple, but the one theme that will come out in all our definitions is this: a disciple participates in the Lord's work; he does not stand on the sidelines watching like a spectator.

THE FIRST-CENTURY FISHERMEN-DISCIPLES

One approach to better understanding terms is to look into the biblical text and to review the historical and cultural context in which Christ's command was made. It was no coincidence that Jesus picked eight fishermen to be among His twelve disciples (John 21). These simple Galilean men were rough and somewhat pedestrian in their thinking. Their Jewish roots, filled with passion and prejudice, often presented challenges to learning new ideas. Despite their obvious skill and success in the fishing community, these practical, hard-working men would soon give up their stinky, hand-woven nets to catch the vision of Christ's ministry. In a similar manner, Jesus is asking each of us to make room in our lives for His calling: to carry out His plan that each one of us begin to disciple others.

Jesus wanted to relate to men who understood the challenges of life in a unique way, men who dealt with the mysteries of nature. He realized that many of the principles, methods, and techniques used in relating to people on a spiritual basis are very similar to those used in fishing. He knew, for example, that a fisherman is always active on the boat. If he's not busy working the nets, he's busy cutting bait or chumming it overboard or adjusting the sails; a fisherman is never idle, and he is no spectator on the job. Jesus knew that this would be a basic requirement of all His disciples, and it was His desire to utilize common everyday men to be among His twelve. By showing the disciples how to apply His teachings, they could then pursue the *ultimate fishing challenge—becoming fishers of men!* Jesus wanted to lead them on the fishing adventure of a lifetime where the rewards have eternal consequences with net-breaking excitement.

> A disciple participates in the Lord's work; he does not stand on the sidelines watching like a spectator.

The Greek word for *disciple* is *mathetes*, which simply means to *learn*. Therefore, a *mathetes* is a learner, a pupil, one who would be considered a student in the truest sense of the word. In the first century an apprenticeship system was used to train spiritual leaders. Those in training attached themselves to a rabbi and literally lived with him. Their goal was both to learn everything the teacher knew and to imitate his way of life. In essence, they so studied his nature, attitudes, and mannerisms that they would eventually begin to mimic their teacher.

If you were to take a trip to Israel, you would see that the Orthodox Jews continue the teaching patterns used during the time of Christ. A senior rabbi enters the room first, followed by others who have the same attire, gait, mannerisms, and hairstyle as the one they are studying. If you will, the followers mimic the person they are following. If the disciple does not apply what he learned, he cannot be counted as a believer. Once again, we see that an apprentice is an active participant in the work of his master; he is no idle observer, sitting on the sidelines watching the master work and taking notes for future reference. No, the true disciple must roll up his sleeves, gird up his loins, and work side-by-side with the master who is teaching him.

The greatest honor a man can give his master is to share with others the joy of his experience and understanding on how to apply the master's teaching to everyday life. When Jesus instructed His disciples to "follow Me," He did not mean to just walk with Him. He meant that these men were to come as close as possible to copying everything that He did, everything that He said, and even the way He said it.

ATTITUDE AND ACTIONS

As I researched the word *disciple*, I found two elements that apply. In order for someone to be a true disciple, he must have a certain *attitude* and resulting *actions*.

The most important attitude that a disciple must develop is the attitude of imitating his teacher. I vividly recall watching one of my fishing buddies as he was teaching his young son how to

> The greatest honor a man can give his master is to share with others the joy of his experience and understanding on how to apply the master's teaching to everyday life.

tie flies. The boy, quite unconsciously, had adopted his father's hunched-over posture as they sat together at the table, and he was scrutinizing every movement of his father's hands, trying desperately to do exactly as dad did. Even the boy's tongue was sticking out of the corner of his mouth, just like his dad! This young fellow had adopted the attitude of a disciple: he was carefully imitating his teacher.

And in this sense, a disciple is also a leader-in-training. Disciples so identify with the master's attitudes and actions that they themselves become leaders. The process begins by receiving Christ as Savior and Lord. When Christ is truly Lord of our lives, we desire to know and be guided by His will and purpose. One then becomes a true learner. A disciple is perpetually learning, growing, and preparing to teach others as he himself matures. Discipleship produces growth and evidence of maturity in wisdom and judgment. A disciple is a learner-in-process who daily becomes more and more like Christ in his thoughts, motives, words, and actions.

But being a disciple requires more than just a correct attitude; it also requires appropriate action. A fisherman does not teach his trade to an apprentice by sitting in a classroom drawing pictures on a blackboard and studying fishing books. A fisherman teaches the art of fishing by doing it! An apprentice might benefit at some point from reading books and studying diagrams, but the basics of fishing—indeed, the most important aspects of fishing—can only be learned by fishing.

Furthermore, these practical lessons can only be learned one step at a time. Because there are so many variables in fishing, repetitive sessions are often needed to thoroughly acquaint an angler with all the possible alternatives. Likewise, a disciple will often learn best by experiencing teaching through custom or habit, hour after hour, day after day, year after year. The eminent Greek scholar Joseph H. Thayer suggested that a disciple is "a special kind of learner—one who learns by use and practice."[2] We function best when we are the same on the weekdays as we portray ourselves on Sunday morning. We need to daily strive towards applying what we believe.

WHY FISHERMEN?

It's interesting to note that more than half of Jesus' disciples were fishermen, including Peter, James, John, and Andrew. What was so special about being a fisherman that lent itself to becoming a disciple of Christ? And how are the attributes of a fisherman transferable to discipling others? Here are a few insights into fishermen that might help us to better understand what it means to be a disciple.

Fishermen are a unique breed and are rarely understood by others. More often than not, dedicated anglers are considered a little odd or eccentric. We all know the stereotype of the avid fisherman, dressed in waist-high waders, plaid shirt, fishing vest with too many pockets, and slouch-style fishing hat—covered from rim to brim with fishing flies and lures. Popular entertainment loves to have fun at the expense of the fishing enthusiast, as he tells increasingly embellished tales of "the one that got away." Some people would find it odd to meet a bass fishing professional who spends two hundred days a year fishing out of a sixty-thousand-dollar boat pulled by a fifty-five-thousand-dollar truck—while living in a single-wide trailer and eating spam for dinner.

Likewise, fishers of men don't lend themselves toward a neat ecclesiastical job description. Every disciple has a different set of talents, gifts, and testimonies that can be used to reach others for Jesus. Every person they approach is unique, like separate species of fish, and each potential disciple of Christ must be approached in a different manner. The gospel of Jesus Christ is always the same, but the presentation to an individual requires the disciples to be sensitive and discerning.

> Fishers of men don't lend themselves toward a neat ecclesiastical job description.

Fishermen keep focused on what they are doing and how it affects their approach to the fish. The fisherman does everything with an intense concentration. Perhaps he needs to wade across a brook to get closer to a fallen tree; he does so with caution and close attention so as not to stumble. He knows that a misstep or a splash or even a sudden shadow might spook the fish away from the place he's trying to get near, and he is always alert to make his moves with care. In the same way, a disciple fixes his eyes on Jesus and uses his Spirit-filled life to tackle each challenge and embrace each relationship as an opportunity to serve his Lord—but his eyes are always fixed on the Master, and his decisions are always based on the Master's Word. It requires concentration and time to properly disciple another person.

Fishermen have faith that every cast will produce a fish. They believe that just one more cast will be the one that produces a trophy fish. Fishers of men live by faith, not by sight (2 Cor. 5:7). This is the same faith Peter demonstrated when he cast his bare hook into the Sea of Galilee and caught a fish with a coin in its mouth (Matt. 17:27). This is also an excellent example of faith in the Teacher and in obedience to His teachings.

Fishermen are passionate and persistent. They will spend countless hours preparing, analyzing, evaluating, and pursuing their beloved sport. They challenge the fish and don't give up. If one strategy doesn't work, then he will try another approach until

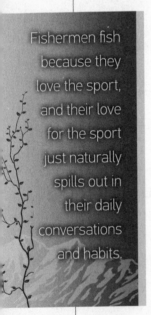

Fishermen fish because they love the sport, and their love for the sport just naturally spills out in their daily conversations and habits.

he can connect with the fish. Similarly, a disciple attacks his mission with the same dedication and zeal; he is alert to opportunities and ready to "cast" at the right moment. If a disciple endeavors to explain some theological point to an unsaved person who isn't receptive, then maybe another approach is required. Some of the best theological points are made through modeling truth and providing practical illustrations of how God's Word can be applied to everyday life.

Fishermen are people of skill and knowledge. They know and study the habits and habitats of the fish while routinely practicing their casting skills. They take the necessary time to prepare for their fishing adventure. Likewise, fishers of men understand the sin-filled environment in which they live and work, while carefully devoting themselves to preparatory prayer and study. Starting your

Trying to live a risk-free life is a form of unbelief.

morning off with prayer and asking God to help direct you to someone who might be open to receive some spiritual advice is a good way to ask the Holy Spirit to help guide and direct your actions, attitudes, and conversations.

Fishermen are eager to share their knowledge, experiences, and skill with others. Fishermen fish because they love the sport, and their love for the sport just naturally spills out in their daily conversations and habits. A fisherman who has tried and been successful in catching fish with a new lure or technique can't wait to share his discovery with his fishing buddies. Similarly, believers are equally interested in sharing the joy of our Lord and Savior with others. We are commanded by our Lord to witness "as we are going." It becomes so much a part of our lives that a "word of the hope that is within us" will naturally flow out of our lives. For as believers, we have the best news of all: eternal life. Let's share that good news so others can discover God's saving grace.

Fishermen take risks and overcome the obstacles before them. Any fisherman can drop his line over the side of a boat and wait for the bobber to move. But the successful sport fisherman knows that bigger fish require more sophisticated tactics; the big fish got bigger simply because they didn't fall prey to the bobber-from-the-boat technique. As a general rule, the greater the challenge, the greater the reward. Many people would not cast a lure into a brush-covered pocket because they might lose expensive equipment—but this is exactly where the accomplished fisherman will cast. He knows that the reward of a "hawg" might be something that others have passed up.

The disciple is no different. A believer must be willing to risk by fishing challenging waters for the bountiful harvest that God has prepared (Luke 5:4). Trying to live a risk-free life is a form of unbelief. Disciples are willing to go out on a limb with the power of the Holy Spirit. Trying to minimize the risk of getting to know new people and sharing your testimony with others is at odds with living close to God.

Fishermen are optimists. They believe in a positive future where every cast will produce the next lake record—or at least a bite. This is part of what makes a fisherman successful, in fact, because

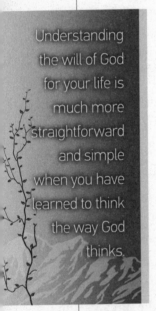

Understanding the will of God for your life is much more straightforward and simple when you have learned to think the way God thinks.

he does not become discouraged and quit whenever he has been skunked during a fishing excursion. In the same way, disciples consider every relationship as being an opportunity to share God's love and grace with their fellow man. He looks for opportunities to engage a person with a caring and compassionate heart. Through the use of metaphors, anecdotes, humor, and sharing his own experiences, a disciple is intentional about connecting with others.

Fishermen catch fish. Finally, both fishermen and disciples understand the central purpose of what they are doing. The purpose of fishing is to catch fish, and the purpose of discipling is to win and mature men for Christ. True disciples don't just fill a pew on Sunday, but are actively involved in "catching others for Christ" (Matt. 4:19).

A BIBLICAL DEFINITION OF A DISCIPLE

While there are many good definitions for the word *disciple*, I believe the best one comes from the apostle Paul in the book of Romans. Let's look at selected verses from Romans 12.

I beseech you therefore, brethren, by the mercies of God, that you present your bodies a living sacrifice, holy, acceptable to God, which is your reasonable service (v. 1). To offer one's body as a living sacrifice means that the disciple must be willing and prepared to let go of all the physical claims that his body might make upon him. This means that the disciple must keep himself pure from the many sins of the flesh, including immoral sexual behavior, drunkenness, and other forms of ungodliness. It might also include times of sacrificing legitimate rest or refreshment in order to be available to help someone else. To be a disciple, a person must first know God and surrender his life to Him completely.

And do not be conformed to this world, but be transformed by the renewing of your mind (v. 2). The "pattern of this world" is to "look out for number one," to love oneself and pursue self-actualization, to climb the corporate ladder and accrue both status and wealth. But notice that Paul does not merely say that we are not to conform to that pattern; he also tells us that the only way of avoiding it is to "be transformed," and this transformation can only come through "the renewing of your mind." In other words, a true disciple of Christ completely changes his way of thinking. He stops thinking the way the world thinks and learns to think as God thinks.

. . . that you may prove what is that good and acceptable and perfect will of God (v. 2). I remember when an employer from my youth told me, "If you have any questions, just ask my assistant

Dave—because he knows my mind." Asking Dave a question was the same as asking the boss, because Dave had learned to think like the boss, and this is part of being a disciple. Understanding the will of God for your life—"that good and acceptable and perfect will of God"—is much more straightforward and simple when you have learned to think the way God thinks. And this is another benefit that we receive as we learn to renew our minds.

Let love be without hypocrisy. Abhor what is evil. Cling to what is good (v. 9). What sorts of hypocrisy tend to creep into human love? This is an apt question for your own meditation, as there are many examples; but one example might be that of double standards. A man might tolerate evil in his own life while abhorring it in his neighbor's life. Paul warns us to establish one firm standard in all areas of our lives and our thinking: abhor what is evil, and cling to what is good. In so doing, we are further renewing our minds to think more and more like Christ.

. . . distributing to the needs of the saints, given to hospitality (v. 13). As the disciple of Christ learns to think like his Master, he also begins to live like his Master, becoming daily more and more like Christ. The disciple is quick to share with those in need, especially to those of the household of faith (Gal. 6:10), and he is quick to open his home to strangers and those who do not yet know the truth of Jesus Christ.

ANOTHER DEFINITION

In 1981 God gave me a vision for developing a ministry directed specifically toward men. Let's Go Fishing Ministries was developed to assist men in becoming the spiritual leaders in their homes, workplaces, churches, and communities (1 Tim. 3). Over the past three decades plus, we have endeavored to better connect with men and assist churches in creating dynamic ministries of spiritual mentoring. As we entered the twenty-first century, a new name was created to better project our role as being a catalyst—a change agent to thousands of churches. Men's Ministry Catalyst (MMC) is a team of multi-talented leaders seen throughout the nation as agents who provoke or speed significant change or action in our church culture. MMC helps stimulate change in men and churches and seeks to inspire, equip, educate, and motivate men to know God more fully so that they can be transformed into the likeness of Christ.

Over three decades later, Matthew 4:19, *"Come,* follow Me, and I will make you fishers of men"* (The Voice), remains as a bedrock focus of the work God has placed before us. Indeed, Jesus' words to His disciples are the rallying point for all Christians. In one simple sentence, Jesus encouraged His disciples to know Him ("Follow Me"), to seek change in their lives that would come from following Him ("I will make you"), and to accept His challenge for the ultimate mission and purpose for their lives: that of discipling others ("fishers of men").

FOLLOW ME

Following Jesus is about being obedient to His commands and the Word of God. To follow Jesus is to recognize that He is the Leader, the Master Teacher, the Supreme Authority, and the Battleground Commander for all of life's spiritual battles. Without His guidance through the power of the Holy Spirit and knowledge of God's Word, we cannot know God's purpose and plan for our lives, nor will we be effective in our Christian walk.

An apprentice, as we have seen previously, cannot hope to learn his master's trade unless he stays close to the master, asking questions and listening attentively to instruction. Or perhaps a better example would be a soldier on the battlefield during the heat of combat. That soldier's very life depends on knowing and obeying the orders of his superior officers—and to know those orders, he must always be in close contact with his commander. Similarly, a disciple must always be in close contact with his Commander in Chief, the Lord Jesus Christ, and this is accomplished through a daily habit of studying God's Word, spending time in meditation and prayer, and constantly asking the Lord to accomplish His will in our lives. As Paul tells us in Romans 12:1–2, the disciple best understands the will of God by renewing his mind, by learning how to *think* the way God thinks.

Following Jesus requires obedience to His Word, just as He taught the disciples: "If you keep My commandments, you will abide in My love, just as I have kept My Father's commandments and abide in His love" (John 15:10). Our God is a jealous God. To follow Christ's teachings means that we do not follow philosophies and beliefs that are contrary to His ways.

I WILL MAKE YOU

Jesus' purpose for His disciples didn't end on the cross. He seeks to have us transformed from the worldly men we are into the likeness of Christ: "For whom He foreknew, He also predestined to be conformed to the image of His Son, that He might be the firstborn among many brethren" (Rom. 8:29).

As already stated, we become transformed as we renew our minds, learning more and more to think as God thinks—and

> A disciple is a person-in-process who, through the power of the Holy Spirit, progressively becomes more and more like Christ.

this process requires that we stay in close fellowship with God. Through the application of Bible study, prayer, Christian fellowship, and meditation on His Word, we allow the Holy Spirit to transform our thoughts, actions, and attitudes so that we properly represent our Master. The more we study His Word, the more His thoughts and desires become an integral part of our own thinking so that our minds stop being conformed to the thinking of the world around us and begin to be transformed into thinking as God thinks. But Christian fellowship is vitally important in this process as well, as a man will tend to become like the people he spends time with. By surrounding oneself with people who value and obey the Word of God, a man will learn by imitation to keep God's Word in the forefront of his life.

True discipleship, then, produces growth and evidence of maturity in wisdom and judgment. A disciple is a person-in-process who, through the power of the Holy Spirit, progressively becomes more and more like Christ.

FISHERS OF MEN

"Do not be afraid," Jesus said to His disciples. "From now on you will catch men" (Luke 5:10). Peter and his fishing partners (Andrew, James, and John) listened to Jesus, obeyed His words, and with faith cast their nets into the Sea of Galilee. The wonder and miracle that they observed caused Peter to collapse at Jesus' feet and recognize Him as the God-man. Peter and the disciples knew that the divine power placed them in the presence of God, for only God could have brought about such an amazing fishing catch. The holy purity of deity brings consciousness of the unholy sinfulness of humanity.

The Greek word translated *catching* in Luke 5:10 is only used one other time in the New Testament: ". . . in humility correcting those who are in opposition, if God perhaps will grant them repentance, so that they may know the truth, and that they may come to their senses and escape the snare of the devil, having been taken captive by him to do his will" (2 Tim. 2:25–26). Notice the striking difference in this second passage, as Paul is telling us that the Devil is the one doing the fishing for men's souls! The disciple of Christ is not simply a fisher of men; he is actually engaged in a desperate tournament for the souls of men, and the competition is from Satan himself.

But this is no ordinary fishing tournament; it's a catch-and-release experience. The idea behind this phrase is that the fisher of men will release his catch, permitting the newly saved disciple to go forth and reproduce. This is an important aspect of Jesus' teachings on discipleship, that all believers are called to be sitting as disciples at the feet of the Master and simultaneously going forth to produce more disciples.

REAL DISCIPLES, REAL SACRIFICE

Jesus elected to use common fishermen to be among a small group of men who would be called to change the world. These ordinary men were trained and educated by our Lord to

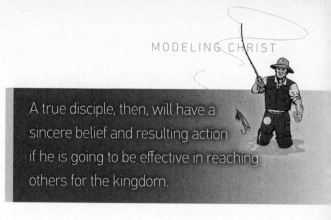

A true disciple, then, will have a sincere belief and resulting action if he is going to be effective in reaching others for the kingdom.

utilize their individual spiritual gifts to help populate a heavenly kingdom. During this period, the disciples lived, worked, and fellowshipped with Jesus. Jesus was a houseguest of the fisherman Peter and his family for at least two years during His three-and-a-half-year ministry. The disciples sat at Jesus' feet and listened to His every word. They studied His methods and adapted His teachings to their everyday life.

In the twenty-first century, however, men find it difficult to live in such close proximity. We persuade ourselves that we are "keeping in touch" with others if we post a sentence or two on someone's social network page, send out a tweet on a mass scale to friends and family, or send a quick text on our cell phone. But this is not the type of discipleship Jesus modeled for us.

Real discipleship relationships require time—lots of time. This is part of the self-sacrifice involved in both being a disciple and offering discipleship to others. It will frequently mean forgoing things you want to do, perhaps dropping something on the spur of the moment because a brother needs help, and many other demands on the commodity that most of us value above all others: time. It might also involve a careful and deliberate balance between time spent on discipleship partners and time spent on family and other high priorities. The one thing it will almost invariably involve is *less* time for yourself.

John Sax, the kiwi friend I mentioned at the beginning of this chapter, believed in the relationship process to help mentor people. He couldn't convince local New Zealand churches to develop an appropriate process for discipleship to happen. So on his own, John started purchasing homes for young men to come and participate in small groups where they would live with a mature Christian who discipled them. John now has several homes that have been used for this purpose; he was "all in" with his resources and commitment to see men grow in the Lord.

To my way of thinking, John exemplifies the essence of a true disciple. He is committed to finding ways to reach others. When his government couldn't find a way to embrace and encourage many struggling young people, John stepped up and formed a foundation (For the Sake of Our Children Trust) to reach young people with the love of Jesus. Countless young people have been saved and discipled, turning away from lives of brokenness and hopelessness to following Jesus Christ.

COUNT THE COST

When on the shores of the Sea of Galilee, Jesus offered His challenge to these respected fishermen. He wanted them to count the cost. "Come, follow Me," Jesus said, "and I will make you fishers of men." In saying "Come, follow Me," Jesus was asking each fisherman to follow and believe in Him. In saying "I will make you fishers of men," He was informing them, "I will now give you a ministry." A true disciple, then, will have a sincere belief *and* resulting action if he is going to be effective in reaching others for the kingdom.

The discipleship concept worked well in the first century, and it still works today. The disciples didn't just learn from Jesus and stop there. They went out and taught others how to fish for souls. The first-century church was filled with passionate people who were "all in," and there were very few standing by on the sidelines as spectators. The blood-laden roads and crosses were filled with people who gave their lives to perpetuate the gospel. Jesus warned His disciples of this very fact, and He commanded them to count the cost before taking on the role of disciples.

In Luke 14:25–33 Jesus told His disciples that following Him and being a committed Christian would possibly disrupt their lives. In my life there was a time when neither my mom nor dad would speak to me for months because I took a stand for my faith. I focused upon the wise words of the psalmist, "My father and mother have deserted me, yet the Eternal will take me in" (Ps. 27:10 The Voice). Bearing our cross (identifying with Christ) requires intentionality and commitment. There will be people and groups who will not include you or accept your ways. Some may even try to discredit you because of your faith. Christ wants us to not only experience the joy of our salvation but also recognize and live through some of the sufferings He felt.

If disciples are sold out for Jesus and He is their passion, followers will want to share their beliefs with others. Discipleship by its nature implies the idea of teaching and encouraging others in their faith. This happens because disciples are available for

> If disciples are sold out for Jesus and He is their passion, followers will want to share their beliefs with others.

relationships and consider every opportunity as a time to build a bridge of understanding to others.

THE ULTIMATE CHANGE AGENT

The process of being changed is what disciples call *transformation,* and transformation is the process of becoming something completely new. A caterpillar, for example, is completely transformed when it emerges from the cocoon as a butterfly, a creature that is utterly and completely different and new. When we transform our minds (Rom. 12:2), we completely change our ways of thinking from the patterns of the world into the pattern of God's mind, and these two ways of thinking are utterly and completely different from one another.

Ed Hindson has inspired me on this topic, and he has brought insights that all of us can appreciate about the process of transformation. First, we must remember that the Holy Spirit is the ultimate change agent. The world that God created is constantly changing. People themselves are in a continual process of change. Living organisms are not static; they are constantly changing. Change comes when people are willing to grow and improve. Change involves several key elements:

Honest view of the past. You won't change as long as you are satisfied with the way things are. Such attitudes may make us content for a while, but they can also leave us unwilling to change when it is apparent change is needed.

Dissatisfaction with the present. There is something wholesome in a holy dissatisfaction with the status quo. Good leaders are always asking how they can improve and make things better. Unless men begin asking the tough questions now, they may wait too long to take action.

Hope for the future. Great leaders are always optimistic about the future. They embrace it and make the most of it. They realize that change is a necessary part of personal improvement.[3]

WHAT IS KEEPING US FROM BIBLICAL DISCIPLESHIP?

I believe our fear of disenfranchisement and lack of faith stands in the way of many Christians becoming "sold out" for Jesus. We fear rejection from those we care about who may not understand the depth of our love and commitment to Jesus. We want to be understood and loved by others, especially our families, and the reality is that being a Christian is sometimes contrary to our culture and the comfort of others.

As Christ recognized the apostle Peter in Matthew 16:15–19 for his faith, we can also be blessed. Peter boldly proclaimed, "You are the Christ, the Son of the living God." Jesus answered and said to him, "Blessed are you, Simon Bar-Jonah, for flesh and blood has not revealed this to you, but My Father who is in heaven" (vv. 16–17). Jesus desires that each one of us be that rock among those struggling souls who have placed their life and values on shifting sands and sinkholes. To recognize that Jesus is our firm and trusted foundation speaks volumes of our commitment and obedience to His Word.

BIBLE STUDY

> I beseech you therefore, brethren, by the mercies of God,
> that you present your bodies a living sacrifice, holy, accept-
> able to God, which is your reasonable service. And do not be
> conformed to this world, but be transformed by the renewing
> of your mind, that you may prove what is that good and ac-
> ceptable and perfect will of God. (Rom. 12:1–2)

Why does genuine transformation require that we renew our minds? What does a man's thinking have to do with the rest of his life? His character?

What does it mean to renew your mind? How is this done? What are the results?

> Then He said to them, "Follow Me, and I will make you fish-
> ers of men." (Matt. 4:19)

What does it mean to become a fisher of men? What things are required of a man if he is to become a fisher of men?

What does it mean to follow Jesus? After one accepts His gift of salvation, what is involved in continuing to follow Him?

MAN UP!

> Fishing for fish is pulling fish out
> of life into death. Fishing for men is
> pulling them out of death into life.
>
> **—Peter Marshall**[1]

TRAINED FOR BATTLE

My good friend Phil Downer serves as president of Discipleship Network of America (DNA), and he is also the author of numerous books, including *Eternal Impact*. DNA is a nationwide network of people committed to following Christ's life of winning and discipling others to become disciple makers.

Phil was a machine gunner who served in Vietnam with the United States Marine Corps in 1967 and 1968, and he is familiar with front-line battles. One day Phil and his company were ambushed by the NVA. During the battle that followed, over 20 percent of Phil's company were killed or wounded. Then suddenly, at the height of the fight, the enemy came up from behind and began firing into Phil's position—meaning he and his buddies were surrounded. Then one of those embarrassing things that can happen in combat inexplicably happened to Phil. Involuntarily, Phil's stomach muscles contracted and he found himself in a fetal position. There are several problems with the fetal position in combat.

✱ It is a very **hard position** in which to operate a machine gun.

✱ Your butt is too high, making you a **bigger target**.

✱ It's simply **embarrassing** as all get out!

But then something happened to interrupt this strange moment. Phil's best friend and squad leader, Ralph, screamed, "I'm hit!" The screams of someone so close to Phil snapped him out of his defenseless position and, in an act of self-sacrificing courage, he took the risk of being exposed to enemy fire by getting up and rushing to help his wounded friend—only to discover that Ralph had harmlessly taken a round through his shirt. To this day Phil and Ralph laugh together about the day that Phil risked his life in combat to save Ralph's shirt! A few months ago while reminiscing about this moment, Ralph said to Phil, "Downer, thanks for coming for me that night."

After coming to his friend's aid, Phil returned to his machine gun and became even more committed to surviving this ordeal. The training and equipping Phil had received from the Marines kicked into action as he relocated his position and returned fire. He recounted that "marines were trained to be fighting men—that's what they do best." They were not designed to be in the safety of the rear command posts with some "donut eaters," but on the front-line battlefield. Marines are fighting men, and they are trained to stay in the battle. That is where their equipment works best, where their training is best fulfilled, and where their lives are most useful.

> The Christian church is full of donut eaters.

And so it is for the Christian soldier as well. The disciple who wants to be used of God in the battle for men's souls is signed up as a career soldier. We are in an ultimate battle for eternal life, fighting for the souls of those who don't know Him. We've been instructed by our Lord to "go out and make disciples" (Matt. 28:19 The Voice), but most Christians have little or no idea what a true disciple is and even less of a concept of how to go about making one. As we saw with Phil's life in the Marine Corps, if we want our lives to count for something beyond our worldly success, there is no time to give up or retreat to the rear with the doughnut eaters.

The Christian church is full of donut eaters. They are the ones who enjoy the church service and then go into the lobby to have their coffee and donuts, but rarely interact at a deep level with anyone. They believe that the pastors and missionaries are the ones responsible for winning souls. They see their responsibilities as financially supporting the church and living a morally good life. They are the spectators of the faith. But believers haven't been called to be spectators. We are called to be in the front lines of the spiritual battle that is consuming our friends, neighbors, and families.

We all believe deeply in something. It could be money, power, fame, work, even ourselves. And most of us are strongly committed to that belief. We believe that we can "pull ourselves up by our bootstraps." We are men, after all! But our lives will not count for much if we do not first and foremost hold a strong, constant, and committed belief in Jesus Christ and His promise that "with God all things are possible" (Matt. 19:26). It is only by making a difference in the lives of other people and helping them become disciples and fishers of men that we will make a difference in the eternal kingdom of God.

JESUS THE REVOLUTIONIST

After Jesus met His disciples He was led by the Spirit into the desert to be tempted by the Devil. Our Lord was tempted in every way imaginable, but He did not give in to the enemy. He held His ground and fought the battle to show His disciples how to deal with temptation, worldly lusts, and fear.

The evil one came to Jesus first on a physical basis, asking Him to miraculously meet His physical needs, specifically the need for food: "If You are the Son of God, command that these stones become bread" (Matt. 4:3). Then Satan appealed to the Lord's emotional side, tempting Him to perform a spectacular, death-defying miracle to show the world that He is greater than death, but doing so without the need to die on the cross: "If You are the Son of God, throw Yourself down. For it is written: 'He shall give His angels charge over you,' and, 'In their hands they shall bear you up, lest you dash your foot against a stone'" (v. 6). And the final temptation came in spiritual form, urging the Lord of creation to bow before one of His own creatures: "All these things I will give You if You will fall down and worship me" (v. 9). Each time, however, Jesus responded to the evil one with scripture. And after these temptations, the Devil left him for a time.

Jesus came as a revolutionary person to challenge the thinking of the establishment. The Pharisees, Sadducees, and priests had everyone convinced that righteousness came by observing the law—not only the Ten Commandments, but a host of other rules and regulations that they had added to God's law. They developed new laws in order to bring people under their control and prove how unrighteous everyone was and how important it was to live a life under the law in order to please God. The convictions of the spiritual leaders portrayed that heaven was a reward for a person's good works and obedience to the law, and this was the fundamental theological position they taught their followers. As Christ entered the scene, He disrupted and challenged the leadership in that understanding as He pronounced that a man is saved by grace and not by works. His claim that we are all cursed and sinful and in need of a Savior left the arrogant elite wondering what was happening to their world.

Jesus knew His disciples well. He had seen them study their trade and apply selected strategies to various situations. Now it was time to transfer those teaching techniques to something far more important than a boatload of fish. It was time to go fishing for souls. And like a disciplined soldier, Christ's troops needed some training, self-discipline, and resources to sustain them through the challenges that every true disciple will face. Matthew recorded Christ's words that would become the "Instruction Manual for Discipleship."

Jesus came as a revolutionary person to challenge the thinking of the establishment.

JESUS' INSTRUCTION MANUAL

Before a soldier goes into battle, he trains and equips himself for the fight. He will determine the magnitude of the job and be sure that he has the necessary resources needed to complete the task. He will instinctively refer back to his basic training, preparing himself for all the combat situations for which he has been trained. He will double-check all his equipment, ensuring that his weapons and armor and communications gear are all functioning in peak condition. What's more, every piece of that equipment has an instruction manual to ensure that the soldier is able to keep it in good working order. These manuals are so designed that even a person with a fourth-grade education can understand the teachings.

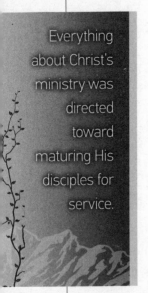

Everything about Christ's ministry was directed toward maturing His disciples for service.

In the same way Jesus equipped His followers with a clear instruction manual, providing them the training they would need as they followed Him into the spiritual combat of our world. The core of this instruction manual can be found in Matthew 5–7, in the passage known as the Sermon on the Mount.

Jesus wanted to invest in men who could make an eternal impact. His desire was to build an army of people who would be warriors for God's kingdom, winning victory over Satan and leading men and women out of darkness and into His eternal kingdom. To do this, a disciple would need to have a battle-ready mind-set that would help him during the tough times. Let's focus on six very specific instructions that Jesus included for His disciples in the Sermon on the Mount.

BE LIKE ME

Disciples are called to be like Jesus. "A disciple is not above his teacher, nor a servant above his master. It is enough for a disciple that he be like his teacher, and a servant like his master" (Matt. 10:24–25). That is the bedrock of discipleship. Those who call themselves disciples are to be like our Teacher, Master, Lord, and King. Remember that a disciple is a leader-in-training, a learner, and he is to have Christ's values and priorities. This theme is a recurring topic in Scripture; the discussion of discipleship is found throughout Christ's teaching because He desires to have people count the cost of following Him. It is fundamental to a person's faith.

Jesus is involved in perfecting the saints for the work of ministry. Men who are transformed are to make disciples who can, in turn, reproduce themselves. Discipleship is apprenticeship. It is the process of sharing, encouraging, modeling, teaching, listening, and serving. Or the disciple can be thought of as a raw recruit in the military who learns a skill by working very closely with his master sergeant. They share living quarters with each other, go to the mess hall together, and work together in the field. The recruit is given some texts to study concerning his position on the team and operation of the gear he is responsible for, but the vast majority of his learning will come through hands-on experience and careful imitation. He learns by watching how the master sergeant and technicians perform their craft, then he tries to imitate that himself in real-life application.

The Christian life is not much different. Everything about Christ's ministry was directed toward maturing His disciples for service. Every man who has been born again into Jesus Christ should be maturing in his faith while also encouraging others.

James, the half brother of Jesus, reminds disciples that they must be doers of the Word and not just hearers (James 1:22). Remember, more people will come to Christ by men modeling God's love than by their words. Believers need to do more than speak the message—in fact, they *are* the message. Transformed people are to accurately imitate Jesus in every way.

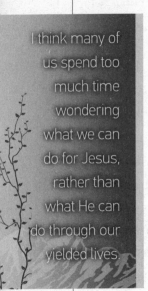

I think many of us spend too much time wondering what we can do for Jesus, rather than what He can do through our yielded lives.

The emphasis of the Holy Spirit is in the being, not the doing. Jesus said, *"Here's the knowledge you need:* you will receive power when the Holy Spirit comes on you. And you will be My witnesses, first here in Jerusalem, then beyond to Judea and Samaria, and finally to the farthest places on earth"* (Acts 1:8 The Voice).

The Great Commission is often misinterpreted with an emphasis being placed upon the doing. However, the primary focus is upon making disciples, not going, baptizing, or teaching. These are the by-products of discipleship. Luke 6:40 provides further encouragement to this point: "A disciple is not above his teacher, but everyone who is perfectly trained will be like his teacher." The question that men must continually ask themselves and each other is, "If men claim to follow Christ, are they showing others their Christlikeness?" Or, to make it more personal, "If I claim to follow Christ, do others see Jesus in me?" Ken Carpenter stated it this way: "Discipleship is a process. God's desire is to etch into our lives the imprint of His son, Jesus. He is responsible for the construction process of making us like Christ. But He needs yielded, available individuals willing to be shaped, molded and carved by His hands."[2]

I think many of us spend too much time wondering what we can do for Jesus, rather than what He can do through our yielded lives. Jesus constantly reminds us that our daily walk is our testimony and that it is about being His witness wherever we are placed. It's not just a Sunday experience. Jesus provided further clarification of this point, reminding us that a disciple will eventually become like his teacher (Luke 6:40).

When transformed people focus upon the character of God and the teachings of Christ, their faith matures. Men should not focus on themselves, what others might think of them, or how others may see them. What is important to understand is how God sees them and how they can better emulate Him in their daily lives.

DON'T BE AFRAID OF THE WORLD

In Matthew 10, Jesus repeatedly tells His disciples not to be afraid. The Lord tries to calm the disciples' fears because they had just heard Him describe a series of troubles and worries. You will be sent out as sheep among wolves (v. 16); beware of men who will beat you in the synagogues (v. 17); you will be brought before kings and governors (v. 18); you will be a prisoner brought to trial (v. 19); your own family will put you to death (v. 21); you will be hated by many (v. 22); and you will be persecuted for your beliefs (v. 23).

A man's fear will strangle the effectiveness of reaching others, much as it did with Phil and his buddies in our opening story. Fear can so grip our spirit that we can be rendered ineffective.

Spiritually speaking, we can use an acronym that FEAR is really False Evidence Appearing Real. If men become man pleasers, they will give up on the ideas of their faith. There will be a temptation to pull back on their testimony and not confront when the situation dictates (Gal. 1:10).

If you are committed to Christ and attempting to be like Christ, then you can expect to be treated as Christ was treated. This is especially true as to how the world will treat you. The world treated Him as though He were the Devil (Beelzebub). "If they have called the master of the house Beelzebub, how much more will they call those of his household!" (Matt. 10:25). But Jesus

If you are committed to Christ and attempting to be like Christ, then you can expect to be treated as Christ was treated.

tells us again not to be afraid, for "I have overcome the world" (John 16:33). Basically, most believing men are afraid to go into the world because of what others might think of their love for the Lord. Jesus tells us that there will be a day when everything will be made right. God will make the truth known. He will reward and vindicate His own. What they need is an eternal perspective.

In today's society committed believers can lose their eternal perspective when they worry about being popular or wise or noble or politically correct instead of confronting an evil world. Whose praise are you seeking? Remember, the praise of men is fickle. The apostle Paul provided some wise counsel for those of us who struggle with wanting to be popular or accepted by the world. "For do I now persuade men, or God? Or do I seek to please men? For if I still pleased men, I would not be a bondservant of Christ" (Gal. 1:10).

Dedicated and committed men need to proclaim their allegiance to Christ in public "on the housetops" (Matt. 10:27). Without being obnoxious, believers should go into the world, leaving the comfortable pew in their churches, and proclaim Him to be the King of kings and Lord of lords. They shouldn't alter their messages and lifestyle for the fear of what other people's reactions might be (Gal. 1:10). The apostle Paul didn't worry about everyone threatening to put him in jail because he had an eternal perspective, not a temporal one.

Discipleship involves identification with Christ in His person and sufferings. Paul had it figured out when he stated that his top priority in life was "that I may know Him and the power of His resurrection, and the fellowship of His sufferings, being conformed to His death" (Phil. 3:10). This is a difficult decision. It is one thing to want to know Christ and the power of His resurrection. It is quite another thing to want the fellowship of sharing in His sufferings. Very few of us want to sign up for suffering, especially the types of suffering that Jesus endured throughout His ministry.

PUBLIC CONFESSION

If men believe that Jesus came to die for their sins, if they believe that His power is greater than men's, if they believe that God is a Father who cares for His children, and if they accept His promise of protection and power, then they will not fear or be ashamed of the gospel. Paul's letter to the Romans testifies to this truth. "For I am not ashamed of the gospel of Christ, for it is the power of God to salvation for everyone who believes" (Rom. 1:16).

"Therefore," Christ told His disciples, "whoever confesses Me before men, him I will also confess before My Father who is in heaven" (Matt. 10:32). Believing men must be willing to confess, agree, and affirm that Jesus is Lord. But the verse does not just mean that I will acknowledge Jesus verbally—it also means that my actions and my attitude will acknowledge Him before a watching and waiting and wanting world. St. Francis of Assisi is attributed with saying, "Preach the gospel at all times. If necessary, use words."

If disciples believe that their faith should be kept a secret, they have missed the purpose of discipleship. Believers need to be genuine in their commitment. Those who believe in Christ show forth their commitment by proclaiming His presence in their lives. Once again, the apostle Paul helped men understand this concept when he challenged the early disciples in Rome, "So if you believe deep in your heart that God raised Jesus from the *pit of* death and if you voice your allegiance by confessing *the truth* that 'Jesus is Lord,' then you will be saved!" (Rom. 10:9 The Voice).

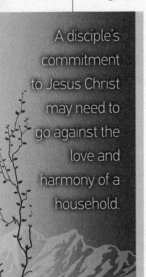

A disciple's commitment to Jesus Christ may need to go against the love and harmony of a household.

A true disciple confesses his faith. Jesus will then affirm His loyalty to the believer by acknowledging before His heavenly Father that he is His child washed in the cleansing blood of the Lamb. Yet even believers can deny their faith in many ways. Their non-Christian actions and attitudes can deny Him. Keeping silent when a testimony is called for can deny Him. Their lack of encouragement to a struggling brother or sister in the Lord can be a point of denial. If transformed people feel a conviction of the Holy Spirit when they have failed in a situation, they need to ask themselves to rethink the response the next time around.

Transformed people will fail in this area. By their nature, they will all have lapses (Rom. 7:15; 1 Tim. 1:15). If they are repentant and broken, they have the heart of a believer. They can ask God for His grace and move on to continue to live a more Christlike life. Many Christians are embarrassed to count the number of times that God provided the perfect opportunity for them to share their faith, but in their silence they denied Him. Thankfully, as a believer matures in the Lord and as we experience the signs of the end times, those times become fewer and fewer.

A COMMITMENT TO DISCIPLESHIP WILL CAUSE DIVISION

Jesus warned His disciples, "Do not think that I came to bring peace on earth. I did not come to bring peace but a sword" (Matt. 10:34). This is a paradox to a believer's understanding. Jesus is in fact the Prince of Peace, yet His presence in a believer's life can split and fracture some relationships. There is peace in those who believe, but to those who do not know Him there will be alienation and rejection toward those who do believe. The sword of conviction and dedication will split many relationships.

The extreme example of this division can be seen in a home. Jesus points out that He will fracture families if necessary. A disciple's commitment to Jesus Christ may need to go against the love and harmony of a household. It doesn't have to be that way, but if it comes to holding on to truth and commitment to discipleship, then disciples must bear the pain of a divided home. The Lord warned His followers that obedience to Him would

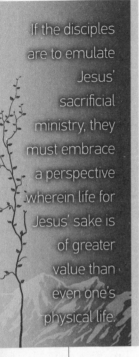

If the disciples are to emulate Jesus' sacrificial ministry, they must embrace a perspective wherein life for Jesus' sake is of greater value than even one's physical life.

cause families to shatter, father turning against son and mother against daughter (Matt. 10:35–39).

Basic conventional thinking and loyalties are shattered by the priority of the kingdom of God as announced by Jesus. There is no neutrality or mutual toleration; one either responds favorably to the message or violently rejects it. The result is that members of a man's own household may be his enemies. Such disruptions are inevitable in households because light and darkness cannot mutually coexist.

In the midst of such conflict and the loss of familial security, it is tempting to compromise one's loyalties. However, Jesus insists that absolute priority must be given to one's relationship with Him, even over family ties. In other words, when the sword of the kingdom results in family divisions, the disciple must make his allegiance clear. The failure to be aligned with Jesus, even against family members, means the forfeiture of one's status as a disciple (v. 37, "not worthy of me"). Jesus' demand of total allegiance on such a personal level is certainly unprecedented within the rabbinic tradition. I have experienced this, and it is probably the greatest pain in my life. I have to constantly ask myself if I wish to be popular with my family or if I want to serve God.

We must remember we live in a broken world. We are all broken, and we need to adjust our expectations of how those who do not have a personal relationship with God judge us or how we judge them. Only God can set the record straight.

The extravagant devotion called for by Jesus in Matthew 10:37 is graphically spelled out in verses 38–39. The vivid metaphorical reference to taking up one's cross captures the imagery of a condemned man forced to carry the means of his own execution. Jesus charges the one who would follow Him to actively take up the cross and follow in a voluntary act of self-denial and obedience. Their solidarity with Jesus demands that the disciples walk the same path of sacrificial obedience. As Donald Hagner noted, "Taking up one's cross refers not to the personal problems or difficulties of life that one must bear, as it is sometimes used in common parlance, but to a radical obedience that entails self-denial and, indeed, a dying to self. To take up one's cross is to follow in the footsteps of Jesus, who is the model of such radical obedience and self-denial (4:1–11)." With these words Jesus provided the most explicit reference to the violent fate that awaited Him.[3] The paradoxical saying of Matthew 10:39 reinforces the message of verse 38 and puts it into proper perspective. If the disciples are to emulate Jesus' sacrificial ministry, they must embrace a perspective wherein life for Jesus' sake is of greater value than even one's physical life. While alignment with Jesus may result in the sacrifice of one's present life, in the end the faithful disciple reaps the reward of eternal life. It is thus in the interest of life in the fullest that the disciple fearlessly faces the prospects of death.

COMMITMENT TO THE CALL

There is one thing even more precious than a man's relationship with his family: the love of his own life. Jesus took His disciples one step further in testing their commitment and dedication. "And he who does not take his cross and follow after Me," Jesus warned, "is not worthy of Me. He who finds his life will lose it, and he who loses his life for My sake will find it" (Matt. 10:38–39). The disciples hadn't at this point heard about Calvary's cross, so what was the cross that Jesus wanted His disciples to bear? The disciples realized that He was talking about dying. They knew that either the Romans or Jews would ultimately kill them for their passion and beliefs.

A mark of genuineness for a true disciple is to forsake self, even to the point of a painful death. Today Christians don't have persecuting Roman soldiers or dens of lions to face. For most people, standing up for their faith is not a really threatening thing. But what if it was a life-threatening issue? What if a power suddenly invaded America and all Christians were asked to leave their faith or die? This is a critical choice for every man to make.

Jesus' teaching is quite clear. If committed men are willing to pick up their crosses and follow Him, they will see the blessings of their ministries. The positive, eternal rewards of their faith will be clear.

Matthew 10:37–38 continues to address the topic of family opposition, making it clear that discipleship must take precedence over all other relationships (compare the even stronger language in Luke 14:26). In this saying we find the first of two references in Matthew to taking up one's cross (16:24). Here the metaphor denotes a readiness to endure family hostility and the violent end to which that ultimately might lead. The final saying, on finding and losing one's life (v. 39), is found in one form or another in all four of the Gospels (Mark 8:35; Luke 17:33; John 12:25). According to Jesus, faithful witnesses who endure martyrdom will find life anew in the kingdom. Those who deny Jesus in an effort to preserve their lives, however, will lose the life that matters most.

There are some things that are all or nothing—and discipleship is one of them.

RECEIVE THE REWARDS OF MINISTRY

Jesus said, "He who receives you receives Me, and he who receives Me receives Him who sent Me. He who receives a prophet in the name of a *prophet* shall receive a prophet's reward. And he who receives a righteous man in the name of a *righteous man* shall receive a righteous man's reward. And whoever gives one of these little ones only a cup of cold water in the name of a disciple, assuredly, I say to you, he shall by no means lose his reward" (Matt. 10:40–42, emphasis added).

As seen in the first five principles, there exists a potential for division and persecution. However, there exists an even greater potential that God would use men for expanding His kingdom. If men are striving to be like Him, when someone receives a Christian, they receive the Lord.

A disciple's character in his speaking (prophet) and living (righteous man) become a source of testimony to the world in which men live. Even the small acts of kindness to the little ones, people young in the faith, will be rewarded by the Lord.

A disciple is in part a determiner of destiny for those with whom he comes into contact. A believer's testimony is the hook that God gives men to fish the ponds of life in order to have the opportunity to catch a soul. Don't deny your past or try to avoid the obvious because you're either embarrassed or threatened by what you were. Within understandable protections you can share your story with others, particularly those who have similar backgrounds or who are going through a similar ordeal.

Christ's disciples need to evaluate the depth of their commitment in light of His Instruction Manual. Are they willing to identify with Him without fear, while publicly confessing and submitting to a point of forsaking family or even losing their own life? That is what Jesus asked of His first-century disciples, and He asks each believer today to consider their own level of commitment to His calling.

Discipleship is the idea of studying and imitating Christ and those who demonstrate a good understanding of what it means to be a follower of the Master.

A transformed man's faith is not to be kept in the closet of the church or his home, but is to be lived out in his daily living. The encouragement Christ gave His followers was to go public with their faith. True believers are to be salt and light to a flavorless and darkened world.

BIBLE STUDY

Read Ephesians 6:11–17.

What does it mean that "we do not wrestle against flesh and blood"? What is Paul saying concerning the life of the Christian?

Review Paul's list of armor and weapons in this passage. What does each do? How is each used?

MAN TO MAN

> When we are called to follow Christ, we are summoned to an exclusive attachment to his person. . . . The call goes forth, and is at once followed by the response of obedience. . . . Christianity without discipleship is always Christianity without Christ.
>
> **—Dietrich Bonhoeffer, *The Cost of Discipleship*[1]**

As Hitler and Mussolini prepared to crash down upon Britain, all eyes looked to the cornerstone of resistance, the stalwart and indefatigable Winston Churchill. As Churchill addressed the House of Commons on June 18, 1940, Europe was in retreat. Holland, Luxembourg, and Belgium had fallen. The French government had fled Paris, and now Adolf Hitler turned his eyes toward Britain. The coming Nazi storm suffocated the British people in a vise grip that left many arguing over past mistakes and the future, and even starting to doubt their trademark resolve.

With a slow growl that occasionally rose to a gentle roar, Churchill delivered a masterful speech. Rumbling through an exposition of the past, Churchill was an example of magnanimity, looking to the urgency of the present rather than shifting blame over past mistakes. Possessing a clear, unflinching vision of the present plight, the lighthouse of Britain stood in the creeping night and dared Hitler to extinguish its spirit.

It was a call dyed in the colors of the Union Jack, the moral fabric of that nation, a powerful reminder for Britain to "brace itself of its duty," and a call to rise to a greatness that would echo throughout history.[2] If you were to summarize Churchill's speech, you would come away with four specific requests he gave to his fellow countrymen:

1. SEARCH YOUR HEARTS FOR THE FORTITUDE TO FACE THE FUTURE.

When I think of people who have fortitude, my attention immediately goes to men who show unexpected courage, moxey, staying power, and guts. One of my favorite stories that speaks of a humble man who had enormous fortitude was the reformer Martin Luther. In April 1521, Luther walked into the presence of Charles V and other powerful persons at the Diet of Worms to answer charges of heresy and to hear a possible death sentence. At that moment, an old knight was heard to say, "Little monk, I like the step you take but neither I nor any of our battle comrades would take it."

Consider that little Augustinian monk who shocked Christendom by his defiance of papal authority and who, at last, stood trial for his life. Even seasoned warriors like this old knight recognized the immense spiritual fortitude that enabled Luther to face his ordeal. During a high moment in the trial, Martin Luther exclaimed, "I do not accept the authority of popes and councils, for they have contradicted each other—my conscience is captive to the Word of God. I cannot and I will not recant anything, for to go against conscience is neither right nor safe. God help me. Amen."[3]

Mentors and disciples alike may face times of persecution for their faith, and the Lord calls us to have the fortitude to stand strong for Him. When we are called to model fortitude because someone is persecuting us for our faith, will we be willing to be strong?

2. STAND YOUR POST; DO YOUR JOB WELL.

My wife and I have visited Italy twice. I'm awestruck with the beauty and amazing artwork of this precious land. Perhaps one of the most interesting sites to be found is just outside of Naples. Excavations at the ancient city of Pompeii have revealed many historical insights and some stirring examples of faithfulness. When Mt. Vesuvius erupted and destroyed the city, many people were buried in the ruins. Some were found in cellars, as if they had gone there for safety. Some were found in the upper rooms of buildings, probably for the same reason.

But one Roman sentinel was found standing at the city gate where he had been placed by the captain, with his hand still grasping his weapon. There, while the earth shook beneath him, while the floods of ashes and cinders covered him, he had stood at his post. There, after a thousand years, his faithfulness was revealed.

That is how faithful we are to be to Jesus and His truth. We are not to be deceived by those who would sway us from the truth. We are to stand firm, strong, and resolute. When Jesus comes, or when we go to meet Him, we are to be found at our post with our weapons in our hands, believing the truth and living the truth.

3. DO NOT BE FEARFUL.

Throughout the Bible we encounter this command: "Be strong and of good courage; do not be afraid, nor be dismayed, for the LORD your God is with you wherever you go" (Josh. 1:9). It is important to recognize this as a command, not merely a suggestion or the equivalent of our modern "have a nice day." God commands His people to reject fear and to replace it with courage and strength, because fear is the enemy of God's people. When a man submits to fear, he stops submitting to the Word of God. In fact some translations record the expression "do not fear" 365 times.

Courage is a matter of both choice and faith. A man might feel the emotion of fear, but he chooses to act in obedience to God's Word and to have faith that God is in control of the situation. These choices are based upon a man's understanding that God is faithful at all times, and He will always honor His Word and keep His promises. When faced with fear, choose to remember that "God is with you wherever you go," and trust that God will bring you through.

4. FIGHT THE GOOD FIGHT—THIS WILL BE OUR FINEST HOUR.

Winston Churchill effectively defined what it means to "fight the good fight" in this very speech: have fortitude and faith in facing the future; stand your post and do your job well; and do not give in to fear. When a man follows all three of these principles, he will be fighting the good fight. As Paul reminds us, "He who sows to his flesh will of the flesh reap corruption, but he who sows to the Spirit will of the Spirit reap everlasting life. And let us not grow weary while doing good, for in due season we shall reap if we do not lose heart" (Gal. 6:8–9). James adds, "Happy is the person who can hold up under the trials of life. *At the right time,* he'll know God's sweet approval and will be crowned with life. As God has promised, the crown awaits all who love Him" (James 1:12 The Voice).

Jesus, like Churchill, challenged his followers to focus on the process of winning a war. The battle that Christ asks each disciple to fight is that of defeating Satan's grip on the souls of lost people.

Disciples are called to have fortitude, stand our posts, defeat fear, and praise God for the victory that is ours through a personal relationship with the living God.

And like Churchill's listeners, disciples are called to have fortitude, stand our posts, defeat fear, and praise God for the victory that is ours through a personal relationship with the living God.

When Jesus called His disciples, He asked them to follow Him. We need to choose to have Jesus lead the attack against those temptations and spiritual battles that we face. To *follow* means that we give up our fleshy desires for control and power and allow God to change our hearts for His purpose, plan, and glory. I have already stated that, typically, men don't do relationships well. We sometimes wrestle with our pride, our passions, our lusts, or with basic character issues. We often seek popularity, yet we don't want to get caught up with spending time cultivating deep relationships. At best we stumble when it comes to having patience with others, especially with women. Most men tend to be fearful of intimacy unless we dominate the moment with our self-centered interest. Yet tucked away in the center of every man's heart is an empty place that can only be filled with the knowledge and Spirit of a loving God who says, "You are My beloved Son, in whom I am well pleased" (Mark 1:11).

Jesus also told His disciples that if they followed Him He would make them into something new. We can only be made into something new if we follow His teachings and allow Him to change our hearts. A true disciple is one whom God is changing into the likeness of Christ. Only Jesus can change our attitudes, motives, and priorities through a supernatural process that makes us into relational people with an eternal perspective.

Leaving behind our past, God seeks to shift us to a vision for being His witnesses. It is through the power of the Holy Spirit and some intentional thinking (and acting) that we can become fishers of men, disciplers of others, so that they may have an eternal relationship with a loving God.

IT'S A PROCESS

We have all heard examples of people who had a divine appointment with God through a "come-to-Jesus moment." God works in mysterious ways, as He did with the apostle Paul on the road to Damascus. Paul, whose name was originally Saul, had been an avid persecutor of Christians wherever he could catch them. His most infamous encounter was with Stephen, as he held the cloaks of the men who stoned to death the church's first martyr (Acts 7:58). Yet one day, while he was walking along the road on his way to persecute more Christians, the Lord Jesus appeared to this hardened man, and in one short encounter brought him out of darkness and into light. It was a truly dramatic conversion—but for most of us, becoming a disciple of Jesus is something that happens more gradually and less dramatically, as part of a divine process, much as it did for the original twelve disciples.

The Great Commission is often misinterpreted because some place the emphasis upon the *doing* instead of the *being*, as we discussed in the last chapter. Our primary focus is frequently upon making disciples rather than on going, baptizing, or teaching—and these are the by-products of *being a* disciple. That change of heart, motives, attitude, and feelings is an internal spiritual transformation led by the Holy Spirit.

THE PROGRESSIVE NATURE OF THE CALL

Jesus called His disciples to an increasingly deep level of discipleship, commitment, and understanding of Himself. In John 1, we see Christ approaching His disciples for the first time and asking them to follow Him. He said, "Come and see" (John 1:39). The disciples first had a period of time to learn from the Master, to watch and work with Him. While they believed in Him as a good teacher or rabbi (*didaskalos*), they were not yet ready to accept Him as their Savior and Lord. The "come-and-see" period was a time when they could test their thinking and refine the depth of their commitment. It was a relational time where Jesus came to know them, and vice-versa. It was fellowship in the truest sense of the word (1 John 1:7). Our Lord shared meals and went fishing with them because that was the relational bridge that He used to build a friendship with these men. Today Jesus wants us to look for relational bridges that lay the groundwork for spiritual mentoring. He wants us to know the person we are trying to reach, and He wants us to develop an appropriate personal process that will intrigue the non-believer to *come and see.*

FISHERS OF MEN

Jesus made a second call to discipleship when He said, "Follow Me, and I will make you fishers of men" (Matt. 4:19). Jesus called the disciples to consider changing their primary focus from fishing for fish to fishing for men. This call occurred after the disciples had spent some time getting to know the Master. He lived with Peter and his family in Capernaum for several months. The disciples heard His messages, saw His miracles, and studied His teachings. Their hearts had been transformed and a relationship established while weaving nets, catching fish, and sitting around many campfires.

Jesus wants us to look for relational bridges that lay the groundwork for spiritual mentoring.

As we mature in our faith and become more aware of the Holy Spirit's influence in our lives, we want to become more like the Master. Our personal motives, attitudes, and habits that are not Christlike seem out of place in our daily walk. It is like wearing another person's shoes: the shoes may fit, but there is a feel and smell that something is now out of place with our new nature.

To walk with Christ you don't have to give up anything but your pride. After the Holy Spirit convicts you of your sin and you repent accordingly, you will want to give up those things that are not appropriate in a child of the King. As part of the process in developing into a mature believer, we can identify with the disciples at this point in time as a *commitment to the call to discipleship.*

Jesus is still calling out for those precious few to follow Him and commit to the calling of being a spiritual mentor (true disciple). Being committed does not necessarily mean you are in full-time vocational service, but the reality is that all Christians are to be in the business of sharing the gospel and their story. When we utilize our spiritual gifts, talents, and passions in whatever environment we are placed, God will allow us to connect with people who are prepared to receive His Word. Again, by definition a true disciple is not only a follower but one who seeks to share the enlightenment he has received with others.

LORD OF OUR LIVES

Next in the process of spiritual development, we find the disciples, or *mathetes,* at a different point in their understanding of what is needed to be a disciple. The process of spiritual maturation continues as they learn the importance not just of having "heaven insurance" (salvation) but also of making Jesus Lord of their lives. In Luke 5 we find Jesus again meeting His fishermen disciples back at their workplace, fishing the Sea of Galilee. Some scholars would argue that this chapter is Luke's account of what happened in Matthew 4:19. While a similar event, this meeting has its own life and place in the process. The disciples at this point may have seen Jesus as their Savior, but they hadn't yet committed to make Him Lord of their lives.

Peter demonstrated this transition of understanding in Luke 5, a shift that is reflected in the terms he uses to address Jesus. He begins by addressing Jesus as *Master* (v. 5), a term that any

147

disciple would use in speaking to his teacher. This was effectively the title *rabbi*, a term that is still used today to describe any Jewish teacher. But then Jesus performed a miracle, demonstrating His authority over all levels of creation, and Peter's response changes dramatically: he falls down at Jesus' feet (v. 8). "Depart from me," he cries out, "for I am a sinful man, O Lord!" In this response, Peter was openly confessing that he was a sinner in the presence of the holy God, humbling himself at the feet of His Lord. He was openly stating that Jesus was now more than just his Master; He was Lord of Peter's life.

At this time in their walk with Jesus, we can see a transformation of their spirit toward *confirming their relationship* that Christ was the King of kings and Lord of lords, not just a good rabbi. Even though at the cross most of the disciples deserted Christ for a short period, each of them came back to the realization that Christ was indeed their Lord.

CONTEMPLATE HIS LOVE

In John 21:19 we see Christ's fourth and final call to His disciples. Jesus shared with Peter the importance of shepherding, loving, and serving others, and He made a prediction on how Peter would die a martyr's death—and then He called His disciples: "Follow Me."

Peter and the other disciples were being asked to stretch their faith one more time. Were they willing to forsake everything and even to face a martyr's death for Jesus? Just how deep would their commitment be to serving and receiving God's love? This part of the process could rightly be called *contemplate His love*.

The progression of the call to follow Christ was now complete. For the first time the disciples could understand and accept that they were responsible to make new disciples and to establish His church. They would receive a new power, the Holy Spirit, who would equip them for ministry. At Pentecost the disciples received the gift of the Holy Spirit, and He enabled them to fulfill their call (Acts 1–2). They were now able to approach discipleship with a whole new commitment and zeal.

LET'S GET REAL

Jesus further encouraged His followers by sharing the blessing of His power: "Go therefore and make disciples of all the nations, baptizing them in the name of the Father and of the Son and of the Holy Spirit, teaching them to observe all things that I have commanded you; and lo, I am with you always, even to the end of the age" (Matt. 28:19–20). When we accept Jesus as Savior and Lord, the Holy Spirit can reign in our hearts and provide us the same power as those first-century disciples. We will be a new creation in Christ Jesus (2 Cor. 5:17). Our old self gives way to our new personality and new way of thinking. Like the disciples, we have a new confidence: "Now when they saw the boldness of Peter and John, and perceived that they were uneducated and untrained men, they marveled. And they realized that they had been with Jesus" (Acts 4:13).

For some reason we tend to undersell the raw passion of our transformational experience in following Christ. For some maybe we have become too liturgical or stoic about our faith. To a degree we put our religious experience in a box. For others we have become so relaxed that we sit back and enjoy being spectators to a program rather than participate at an emotional level.

We will go to sports events and yell our heads off, jump up and down, and generally get excited. We aren't ashamed of our passion and zeal for what we believe. Today it's hard to get Christians to show up at a polling place to vote for the traditional Judeo/Christian values this country was founded upon. Christians—where is our excitement and joy for what Christ has done for us? If you are in a church that has a hard time getting excited about evangelism and discipleship, then start a reformation movement of people who get it.

Through our faith we are united and committed to Him. Our goals and passion should be the same as those Israelites who

We tend to undersell the raw passion of our transformational experience in following Christ.

were challenged by the prophet Jeremiah: "Behold, I will send for many fishermen,' says the LORD, 'and they shall fish them'" (Jer. 16:16). More specifically, "I will give the commission to many." Jeremiah was using the image of fishers and fish in a good sense to describe the Jews' restoration. He implied that, just as their enemies were employed by God to take them in hand for destruction, so the same shall be employed for their restoration. So, spiritually, those once enemies by nature were employed by God to be heralds of salvation, catching men for life.

Are you rigged and ready to go fishing? Is your spiritual life in order? Have you progressed in your discipleship, or are you still watching others fish? Are you sitting on the bank as a spectator rooting folks along without any personal involvement?

Accept Jesus as your guide and open your life to being a proactive, intentional disciple of the King. God may not be leading you into full-time ministry, and that is alright; you have plenty of ministry opportunities right where He has placed you. At work, at home, and within your community are people whom only you can reach. Disciple others, take up your cross, and follow Him!

WHAT ARE WE CATCHING AND WHOM ARE WE REACHING?

The Bible states that prior to receiving Christ as our Savior and Lord we were all spiritually dead (separated from God). We were similar to a fish swimming around in the ocean with no plan, purpose, or destination. The fish is lost, confused, and floundering. He is particularly vulnerable to attacks and being led to dangerous attractions. An unbeliever is also lost and confused. They are open to the worldly attractions that can lead them into spiritual death. The fisherman's goal is to catch those lost fish and release them to reproduce. A fish that is caught and released can pass along the lessons learned to other fish.

Scripture implores us with these powerful words:

And you He made alive, who were dead in trespasses and sins, in which you once walked according to the course of this world, according to the prince of the power of the air, the spirit who now works in the sons of disobedience, among whom also we all once conducted ourselves in the lusts of our flesh, fulfilling the desires of the flesh and of the mind, and were by nature children of wrath, just as the others. But God, who is rich in mercy, because of His great love with which

He loved us, even when we were dead in trespasses, made us alive together with Christ (by grace you have been saved). (Eph. 2:1–5)

From this verse we get a clearer definition of what it means to be separated from God:

✳ Living in your "trespasses and sins"

✳ Following "the course of this world"

✳ Following "the spirit who now works in the sons of disobedience"

✳ "Conduct[ing] ourselves in the lusts of our flesh"

✳ Prideful and stuck on doing their own thing

✳ "Fulfilling the desires" of your sinful nature[4]

Those who are spiritually dead often share certain traits: unbelief, lack of conviction, hard hearts, a feeling of hopelessness, rebellion about things of the Lord, and acceptance of the things of this world. They refuse to place control and accountability in anyone but themselves. They reject the notion that God's will should be paramount in their thinking and planning. Many nonbelievers have been deceived by the evil one and the false teachers and prophets of this age.

Things weren't much different with the people in Corinth, Rome, Ephesus, Colosse, or Galatia as the apostles approached the unbelievers. Paul asked the Ephesian believers to pray for him, "that utterance may be given to me, that I may open my mouth boldly to make known the mystery of the gospel, for which I am an ambassador in chains; that in it I may speak boldly, as I ought to speak" (Eph. 6:19–20).

WHAT DO SPIRITUALLY DEAD PEOPLE NEED?

* A recognition that we all start out spiritually dead

* An explanation of the gospel

* To see the gospel lived out (modeled by those who really know Jesus)

* Answers to their questions about the Bible, God, Christianity, and so on.

* Believers to pray that the Holy Spirit will draw them to Christ

* An invitation to receive Christ

The Bible shows us different examples of the spiritual maturation process. An interesting perspective comes from the apostle John. In his first epistle John wrote:

> I write to you, fathers, because you have known Him who is from the beginning. I write to you, young men, because you have overcome the wicked one. I write to you, little children, because you have known the Father. I have written to you, fathers, because you have known Him who is from the beginning. I have written to you, young men, because you are strong, and the word of God abides in you, and you have overcome the wicked one. Do not love the world or the things in the world. If anyone loves the world, the love of the Father is not in him. For all that is in the world—the lust of the flesh, the lust of the eyes, and the pride of life—is not of the Father but is of the world. And the world is passing away, and the lust of it; but he who does the will of God abides forever. (1 John 2:13–17)

THE PLAN

THE SPIRITUAL CHILD (NOVICE FISHERMAN)

It is interesting to note that when a child is first born he doesn't really know who his father is. The world is a big mystery; however, through fellowship babies come to know their earthly fathers. They see and begin to understand his life, his faith, his passions, and his hope. As they mature into young men, they begin to make choices about life and their future. Sometimes those choices are good and sometimes not so good. Either way they have to live with the choices they make and take responsibility for the consequences of those choices.

In a similar manner John defines for us a process of spiritual maturity that leads to knowing the divine Parent. As spiritual infants we are characterized by ignorance, confusion, and dependence. We lack clarity and discernment concerning biblical truth. Often we mix several religions into our thinking because

Christian fellowship brings people closer to God.

it suits our lifestyle. Confusion can settle in as we endeavor to replace the faith of our fathers with new habits, attitudes, and thinking that might lead us down the wrong path.

As spiritual children we desire to know how to become true disciples of Jesus. We have a dependence and need because some spiritual growth can't come in isolation. We need help! God's Word, the Holy Spirit, prayer, and spiritual mentors are needed to help us sort out our theology, emotions, and lifestyle.[5]

A spiritual infant needs to be loved, encouraged, and fed in order to grow. Peter put it this way: "So get rid of hatefulness and deception, of insincerity and jealousy and slander. Be like new-born babies, crying out for spiritual milk that will help you grow into salvation if you have tasted *and found* the Lord to be good" (1 Peter 2:1–3 The Voice).

As we disciple spiritual infants, it is good to keep in mind that they need personal attention; they are vulnerable to spiritual attacks and must be protected. Remember, they will model what they see in other Christians, and they need a game plan on how to live a Christ-centered life.

THE SPIRITUAL YOUNG MAN (OCCASIONAL FISHERMAN)

A spiritual mentor can assist an immature believer by helping him find God's plan and purpose for his life. As they mature they begin to explore the gifts and talents God has given them so they can serve and assist others. As we analyze the traits of a young man, we often see they can be over-confident, self-indulgent, idealistic, or naïve; but they are also young warriors in the faith. They will fight battles they believe in. Young men active in the life of a church can offer much to its vision and vibrancy. They bring a host of fresh ideas and approaches to discipleship that the older guys might not have tried. They see their culture through a different lens than the older generation and usually have some pretty good ideas on how to reach that culture.

The more mature Christian needs to help younger men approach their dreams with the appropriate amount of caution but not enough to throttle their enthusiasm and passion. As Scripture reminds us, young men are strong and able to fight spiritual battles that would wear out many older guys. Mature believers need to be encouragers and balcony fans of the younger guys. It is helpful to remember that today many of the young men have grown up in a household without a biological father present. They need the older guys to be the role models and influencers that help them walk through the mine fields of disappointment and discouragement.[6]

THE SPIRITUALLY MATURE MAN (PRO ANGLER)

Spiritually mature men are like parents or adults—they tend to reproduce and they need to leave a legacy. They become involved with seeing others come to know Jesus. They are spiritual mentors and look for ways to share their experiences, their mistakes, their victories, and truths that transform lives. They are men who can see over the horizon and help a child or younger man see the minefields of life before they experience the devastation of failure and defeat.

We are in need of all three phases of men discipling others; the most effective discipler/mentor is a man who has been around long enough to experience both the victory and defeat life brings. A spiritually mature person works hand in glove with God to help men assess and evaluate life at a deep level. When a person has reached a point in life where he cares more about what God says to him than what man says (Gal. 1:10), he is no longer trying to impress the world with his skills and knowledge but is happy to serve our Lord.

No man can stand alone; but spiritually mature men are self-starters or self-feeders in the Word so that the Holy Spirit can lead and direct their lives. They study and apply God's Word in their daily living and habits. Their study is self-driven rather than guilt or pastor driven. The spiritual battles they fight and the disappointments they endure are seen as companions in the maturing process. These experiences help humble their spirit while they seek new ways to give God the glory and praise and credit for their successes. They tend to focus on building a life of significance, not just a life measured by power, fame, and fortune.[7]

The writer of Hebrews gave some warning to those who believe they are spiritually mature men: "Beware, brethren, lest there be in any of you an evil heart of unbelief in departing from the living God; but exhort one another daily, while it is called 'Today,' lest any of you be hardened through the deceitfulness of sin" (3:12–13).

NEVER GIVE UP

Winston Churchill was sixty-six years old when he delivered his famous speech to parliament in 1940. He shared an important trait with many of the prophets of the Old Testament: they were in their latter years when they did some of their most important work for God. The same is true for many of the early patriarchs like Abraham and Moses.

Noah was six hundred years old when the great flood destroyed mankind (Gen. 7:6). Abraham was one hundred years old when Isaac was born (the child of promise). Jacob (Israel) was 130 years old when he and all his family moved from Canaan to Egypt due to the famine in the land (Gen. 47:9).

Moses was approximately eighty years old when he returned to Egypt to face Pharaoh and lead the Hebrew nation out of bondage (Ex. 3–5). Remember, he had just spent forty years tending sheep on the backside of nowhere.

Joseph (a prototype of Jesus) was thirty years old when he became second in command in Egypt (Gen. 41:46). Jesus was approximately thirty years old when He began His public ministry (Luke 3:23). God uses men in mighty ways throughout their lives, as they remain committed to Him.

The sea of our nation is full of the spiritually lost. We need more fishermen, more disciples, for Jesus to harvest the catch. Some will say, "I'm really not prepared to go fishing." Take what knowledge and experiences you have and give it a shot.

BIBLE STUDY

Read Joshua 1:1–9.

☐ Why does God keep repeating the command "be strong and of good courage" in this passage? Why are strength and courage important for a follower of Christ?

☐ What does it mean to "be strong"? How is this done in practical terms?

☐ What does it mean to "be of good courage"? How is this done in practical terms?

☐ What part do faith and determination play in avoiding fear?

MAKING A DISCIPLE

10

> Discipleship is the process God uses to conform us into the likeness of His Son. Our response to the Holy Spirit's convicting and convincing voice is our gift back to a loving Father.
>
> **—Jim Grassi**

As part of our ministry to men, we provide a number of Pastor's Workshops and Iron Sharpens Iron Men's Equipping Conferences. At the end of a 2011 ISI Conference in Sacramento a middle-aged man came up to us and said, "I'm the chaplain at the Solano State Prison and would really like to have a conference like this at our prison. Would you ever consider providing a conference for us?" We knew he had no resources to fund such an event and yet we recognized the need to be responsive to this request. After some discussion and prayer with our staff, we called Chaplain Tim and said we were willing to provide the conference.

The chaplain wanted a full-day program at two of the three facilities within the complex. The offenders were men who had been jailed for five years to life. After we went through two security checkpoints, the electronic iron door closed behind us. The guard said, "You're on your own now! If things go to pot and you actually have a chance to blow the whistle I've given you, we will try to get you out." For myself and my CEO who grew up on the streets of East Oakland, it wasn't much of a comfort that all that stood between us and some murderers was a little red whistle.

The recreation hall where we gathered was filled with industrial furniture and a small sound system. Just as we were unpacking our briefcases, a horn sounded and the doors opened. Scores of prisoners walked in to listen to and evaluate what we would share about our beloved Savior. And that they did.

The Holy Spirit filled the rooms on both days as we saw many men come to faith or re-dedicate their lives to Christ. Healing happened as we explored God's Word about conflict resolution and spiritual healing. There was something special about those two days. The eagerness of the men to receive what God had prepared in our hearts was humbling. Unlike some audiences outside prison, the men weren't looking at their watches to see when the service would end, they didn't have cell phones and iPads to distract them, and they actually brought note pads and pens to take notes. Many men stayed to chat with us about their vision and plans once they got out of prison. They truly appreciated the information and sought a deeper relationship with the living God.

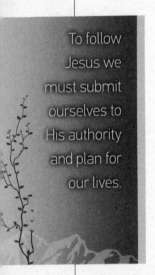
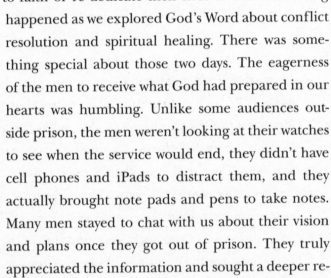

To follow Jesus we must submit ourselves to His authority and plan for our lives.

A year later, we were providing a pastor's workshop to a group of inner-city pastors. The praise and worship during this program was powerful and emotional. Many of the African-American pastors at the conference had been struggling with

> There needs to be a time of preparation and equipping if you are going to have an impact as a discipler of other men.

how to capture the hearts of young black men who get involved in destructive activities during their youth. We had the privilege to share how God could change hearts and even communities.

At the close of our presentation, a middle-aged African-American man came up to us with tears in his eyes and said, "I'm here today to learn more about becoming a full-time men's ministry pastor. Last year, you came to the prison where I had been an inmate for many years. Your inspiration and the power of the Holy Spirit transformed my life. Now I'm a free man and I want to become a good role model for other guys struggling with the issues that got me into trouble." As he spoke, the emotion in his voice strongly conveyed his love and commitment to his mission of being a spiritual mentor for Jesus with inner-city men.

In previous chapters I covered what it meant to be a disciple of Jesus and the relational process He used to call the Twelve. To follow Jesus we must submit ourselves to His authority and plan for our lives. We no longer live for self; rather, we strive to become spiritual mentors (fishers of men) through His Word, the power of the Holy Spirit, the open doors of opportunity in our lives, and the fellowship of other believers.

In this chapter we will discuss some of the attributes needed to be a balanced and effective spiritual mentor. Much like the man at the pastor's workshop, there needs to be a time of preparation and equipping if you are going to have an impact as a discipler of other men. There is the preparation period when your spirit, attitudes, and spiritual gifts are transformed into a witness that attracts people to being a disciple of Christ.

RELYING ON THE HOLY SPIRIT

Abraham Lincoln once stated, "I will study and prepare myself and someday my chance will come."[1] Similarly, spiritual mentors have a responsibility to prepare for ministry. We are instructed, "Therefore gird up the loins of your mind, be sober, and rest your hope fully upon the grace that is to be brought to you at the revelation of Jesus Christ" (1 Peter 1:13). For you, the Holy Spirit is standing by, the Master Teacher, ready to aid you in preparation so that you can make a difference in the lives of other men, as well as in your family, your community, and the kingdom of God. Your responsibility is commitment to the task.

We must also rely on the Holy Spirit to prepare the person we hope to disciple by convicting and enlightening his heart (John 16:8–11). When this has been done, the person becomes open to receiving truth and encouragement. Sometimes in our zeal to disciple others, we try to assume the responsibilities of the Holy Spirit. This often leads to frustration and confusion. Remember, no individual has ever single-handedly brought another person into the kingdom. The Holy Spirit must be the prompter (John 6:44).

A FOUR-STEP CHECKLIST TO PREPARE FOR SPIRITUAL MENTORSHIP

As we review Christ's life and teachings, there is a clear pattern that precedes His major presentations to the multitudes. He was always balanced, rested, focused, and mindful of God's power. We see similar qualities reflected in the opening verses of Psalm 23. In fact, these verses set forth a four-step checklist that can help disciples become more effective in preparation and in the presentation regarding ministry opportunities.

STEP ONE: REMEMBER THAT JESUS IS LORD

The psalmist said, "The LORD is my shepherd; I shall not want" (Ps. 23:1). Disciples of Christ need to recognize and acknowledge that Jesus is Lord. If we are to be effective in our discipling, He must be preeminent in our thinking and actions. Because He is the sovereign Lord, He is truly a worthy shepherd. There are many comforting verses that speak of the Lord's sovereignty. The psalmist said, "I will go in the strength of the Lord GOD; I will make mention of Your righteousness, of Yours only" (Ps. 71:16). We are reminded by the psalmist that "The LORD has established His throne in heaven, and His kingdom rules over all" (Ps. 103:19).

STEP TWO: REMEMBER THE IMPORTANCE OF REST

The psalmist said of Christ our Shepherd, "He makes me to lie down in green pastures" (Ps. 23:2). Christ often withdrew from the multitudes to rest physically and prepare His heart in quiet meditation before presenting His major messages (Matt. 14:13; Mark 6:31; Luke 4:42). Most often He was near the majestic Sea of Galilee where He could ponder God's infinite creation and revive His weary body with sleep and relaxation. Rest was a high priority for Him.

Rest should be a high priority for us as well. Indeed, physical rest is crucial to reducing stress and balancing out our body chemistry. Without rest we deteriorate. That is why Christ's ministry of enabling us to "lie down in green pastures" is so vitally important. Too often, in our well-intentioned efforts to disciple someone, we approach them with near empty cups because our own spiritual lives are in need of refreshment. We try to help someone when we are tired, short of time, or grumpy. People sense those qualities, so it is important that we prepare ourselves with the right attitude and disposition. Good disciples are rested disciples.

STEP THREE: REMEMBER THAT SPIRITUAL REFRESHMENT IS VITAL

The psalmist said of Christ our Shepherd, "He leads me beside the still waters" (Ps. 23:2). In our zeal as modern-day spiritual mentors, we often try to measure the effectiveness of our relationships and ministry according to the volume of activity, according to the number of contacts we have. God's design for our witnessing is that it would not be burdensome or detract from those quiet moments that can quench the thirst of our spirit (Matt. 11:28).

In properly preparing to minister (or fish), many of us forget to seek out the quiet waters of life where inspiration and refreshment abound. Many of us are in the fast lane of life and would like to pull over at the next rest stop where we can obtain needed refreshment. How foolish it is to ignore our stress-filled lives, because stress is the built-in pressure gauge that God has given us to help us limit our activities and develop deep relationships.

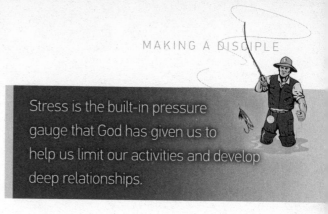

> Stress is the built-in pressure gauge that God has given us to help us limit our activities and develop deep relationships.

Some who refuse to pull over from the fast lane will find their physical or emotional engines blowing up. They will be forced to the side of the road. We need to take spiritual refreshment seriously. If we don't, we pay the consequences.

STEP FOUR: REMEMBER THAT GOD GUIDES AND DIRECTS US

When Christ is at the center of our lives, our desire is to order our priorities so that we follow His prescription for wellness. It is then that our spirit is sensitive to His guidance and direction.

The psalmist tells us that Christ our Shepherd will guide us "in the paths of righteousness" (Ps. 23:3). He will lead us, He will direct us, and as we follow His lead our lives become balanced and unstressed, focused in on God's plan for our lives.

A DISCIPLE IS ALWAYS PREPARED

Followers of Christ prepare for opportunities to share the good news of the gospel with others. We are admonished, "But sanctify the Lord God in your hearts, and always be ready to give a defense to everyone who asks you a reason for the hope that is in you, with meekness and fear" (1 Peter 3:15).

One prepares for those God-given opportunities through prayer, memorization of Scripture, and a keen awareness of the leading of the Holy Spirit. We must stay in close contact with the Christ who saved us and sent the Holy Spirit to be our teacher, counselor, and guide (John 14:26).

THE PLAN

A spiritual mentor needs to have a positive, affirming, and even competitive attitude to be an encouragement to the unbeliever. We must be excited about the "product" we have to share—the gospel that leads to eternal life. Ephesians 4:23 indicates that a proper attitude comes from the Holy Spirit and by studying God's Word. Believers are encouraged to "be renewed in the spirit of your mind" (Eph. 4:23). The attributes of confidence and unselfishness are to be woven into the fabric of our character.

Scripture also tells us that we are to model the attitude of Christ in our daily lives (Phil. 2:5). Indeed, Paul said, "fill your minds with *beauty and* truth. Meditate on whatever is honorable, whatever is right, whatever is pure, whatever is lovely, whatever is good, whatever is virtuous and praiseworthy" (Phil. 4:8 The Voice). As disciples, it is imperative that we have an open and loving heart that manifests itself with an infectious attitude that attracts people to Christ who is working in and through us.

ACTING WITH KNOWLEDGE

An excellent example of acting with knowledge comes from the arena of fishing. For many men, fishing and hunting are very important and they spend a great deal of time reading up on the latest information in their particular field. A seasoned angler studies various techniques and theories that can be used in improving his stringer. Every day new scientific discoveries come to light that help him better understand the nature, character, and environment of fish. A good fisherman studies all available information and applies it to each given fishing situation.

Only a foolish and prideful fisherman or disciple ignores the quest to discover new truths. Solomon once said, "Every prudent man acts with knowledge, but a fool lays open his folly" (Prov. 13:16). A discerning heart will seek knowledge in order to become equipped for service (Prov. 15:14). A committed disciple will call out as the psalmist did, "Teach me good judgment and knowledge" (Ps. 119:66).

A disciple prepares himself by studying the Word of God, while continually exploring new ways to present the truth. The Bible has the answer to virtually every question we can ask. We are encouraged to ask of God when we lack wisdom, for our Lord "gives to all liberally and without reproach" (James 1:5). Prior to being martyred during the reign of the Roman emperor Nero, Peter penned these encouraging words to his disciples: "but grow in the grace and knowledge of our Lord and Savior Jesus Christ. To Him be the glory both now and forever. Amen" (2 Peter 3:18).

MAINTAINING PATIENCE

Scripture teaches us that it is the job of the Holy Spirit to prepare a man to receive the good news (1 Cor. 2:11, 13–14). However, it is the responsibility of each disciple to pray for the appropriate time to share God's Word. So often spiritual mentors make a single feeble attempt to share truth with a friend or neighbor and then become discouraged because their message was not initially received well. We quickly become disappointed with those who seem uninterested in God's Word. This is especially the case when we share our faith with relatives or close friends. It is admittedly difficult to discuss matters of spiritual significance with those who are closest to us. We often make the excuse that we tried once to share God's Word and failed to create any interest, so why try again? Have we really tried all the avenues that could have been explored? Did we persevere with patience? The apostle James reminds us that those who persevere with patience yield results in the end (James 1:12). As disciples, we should always be patient as we approach each challenge and opportunity.

Throughout this book I have drawn an analogy between fishing and discipling. I see the fisherman in this analogy as a spiritual mentor. The fish is equivalent to the person who is lost—a person without Christ. The rod and reel may be likened to spiritual gifts—the equipment that God gives His disciples. The line connecting the rod and reel to the lure is the Holy Spirit. The lures within a tackle box are the various testimonies and experiences God has given each of us.

THE RIGHT EQUIPMENT

In preparing for a day's fishing, a master fisherman thoughtfully selects the necessary equipment for his trip. Careful attention is given to details. Only equipment that is clean and operating efficiently will be selected. This minimizes the potential for disruption or frustration due to equipment failure.

The most important equipment a fisherman needs is his rod and reel, the fishing line, and a good assortment of lures. Without these basic tools he would find fishing very frustrating, if not impossible. Just as a fisherman needs the right equipment to fish, so a spiritual mentor must have the right equipment for the specific task that God has set before him. In what follows, we shall draw some analogies between the fisherman's equipment and the equipment used by the spiritual mentor.

ROD AND REEL: SPIRITUAL GIFTS AND NATURAL TALENTS

The rod and reel are very important to the success of a fisherman. The make or quality of the gear is not nearly as important as knowing how to use each item effectively. A rod must be sensitive enough to feel the light bite of a timid fish while sturdy enough in the butt section to set the hook into the jaw of the fish. Selection of a rod should be based on the species one is attempting to catch and the type of fishing one wishes to pursue. Despite the size, though, the most important thing is that the rod and reel be properly balanced with the line, lures, and angler's level of competence.

> Our gifts are to be used as functioning equipment that can enable the Holy Spirit to work within and through us.

Just as there are different types of rod and reel combinations, so there are a variety of spiritual gifts. "There are diversities of gifts, but the same Spirit" the apostle Paul tells us in 1 Corinthians 12:4. Each of us has "gifts differing according to the grace that is given to us" (Rom. 12:6). These gifts include serving, teaching, encouraging, contributing to the needs of others, leadership, and showing mercy (vv. 6–8). Other gifts are listed in 1 Corinthians 12:1–11.

The body of believers needs all the spiritual gifts in order to function effectively. Our gifts are to be used as functioning

Did you ever stop to think that God can use you in reaching others who share your circumstances, experiences, and ambitions?

equipment that can enable the Holy Spirit to work within and through us. Regardless of what spiritual gifts we may have, they are all to be used in honoring and serving our Lord. As the apostle Peter put it, "As each one has received a gift, minister it to one another, as good stewards of the manifold grace of God" (1 Peter 4:10).

God has also given each of us specific talents. In what areas are you talented? God can use these areas for His glory. What are some areas of interest, hobbies, vocations, avocations, struggles, victories, afflictions, and healings that are unique to you? Did you ever stop to think that God can use you in reaching others who share your circumstances, experiences, and ambitions? He can and He will! Among the adventures that shaped my life have been three brushes with death. At the age of thirty-seven I had a nine-and-a-half-hour brain surgery for a nonmalignant tumor that could have taken my life. God provided two very gifted surgeons who demonstrated great skill, wisdom, and patience to perform this amazing surgery, leaving me with minimal side effects.

On two separate occasions I was involved with incidents on private planes that could have taken our lives, including a crash landing and a mechanical failure. Once again, God spared me from the grip of death.

Depending upon the situation, when I'm listening to people about their dilemma, I draw upon the emotions and thoughts I experienced in my adventures. Not all my stories deal with life or death experiences. By using stories I endeavor to connect with people about their situations to help them understand that God has a plan and will use their challenges to develop great character and to provide a testimony they can share with others.

Each story in my life can help me connect to someone who has a similar issue or challenge. If used properly, it's like picking the perfect lure for the right situation in tempting a fish to bite your bait. Each lure has its proper purpose, actions, color, shape, and size that can be very productive in connecting you to a fish. A person whom you are discipling may be drawn to you and Christ through some little story that testifies to God's faithfulness in your life and how He delivered you from some situation.

If we are to be truly effective spiritual mentors, we must meet people in the marketplace of life and use both our spiritual gifts and our talents to share the greatest news of all—salvation in Jesus Christ. What are some of the things you have faced that shaped your personality, character, faith, and vision? How might you share those stories with others?

FISHING LINE: THE HOLY SPIRIT

It is imperative that a master fisherman continually check and restore his fishing line. The line is the vital link between the rod and reel and the lures. There are a variety of lines, and the quality varies with the cost of the product. It is important to always have enough good line on your reel to provide the best possible chance of catching that fish of a lifetime.

Most major manufacturers produce fishing lines that are abrasive-resistant and minimize line stretch. These are important factors that affect the setting action on the fish. Lines should be frequently checked and replaced, particularly after heavy use or when fishing around abrasive objects such as trees, rocks, and brush.

As a fisherman depends on good line, so a disciple depends on the Holy Spirit. A disciple must constantly walk in dependence upon the Holy Spirit for guidance, direction, and wisdom (Gal. 5:16). The Holy Spirit is the divine enabler who empowers us to use our gifts (rods and reels) and testimonies (lures) effectively as we relate with others.

John the Baptist prophesied that Jesus would come and baptize with the Holy Spirit (Luke 3:16). This was ultimately fulfilled on the day of Pentecost (Acts 2). Since that time, every believer experiences the baptism of the Holy Spirit (1 Cor. 12:13). Prior to sending out His disciples, Christ spoke of the importance of the Holy Spirit as an encourager and teacher: "But the Helper, the Holy Spirit, whom the Father will send in My name, He will teach you all things, and bring to your remembrance all things that I said to you" (John 14:26).

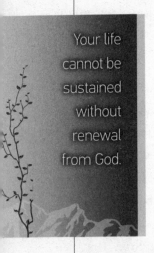

Your life cannot be sustained without renewal from God.

A spiritual mentor needs to be filled regularly with the Holy Spirit (Eph. 5:18). The daily challenges of life are sometimes abrasive and demanding to our supply of the Spirit. Through ministering to others we periodically empty our spool of resources and need to be refilled with the Spirit so that we can continue to serve our Lord. Your life cannot be sustained without renewal from God.

It is essential to replace the body's energy by eating, sleeping, and exercising. Similarly, the Christian cannot function without his soul being revitalized by reading God's Word (as illuminated by the Holy Spirit), listening to Spirit-filled Bible teaching,

Just as good bait attracts a fish, so we can attract unbelievers to the Lord by our vibrant testimonies.

and participating in the soul-filling table of Communion. The prophet Isaiah urged, "Let the people renew their strength" (Isa. 41:1).

Part of revitalizing our lives involves taking time to be still and listening to God (Ps. 46:10). In humble prayer, draw near to the footstool of His divine mercy, and realize the fulfillment of His promise: "But those who wait on the LORD shall renew their strength" (Isa. 40:31). He will always hold us as the object of His infinite affection and encouragement.

THE TACKLE BOX AND THE LURES: OUR TESTIMONIES AND LIFE EXPERIENCES

A good fisherman will have different baits and lures that can be used to catch a variety of fish in different situations. Each fisherman has his favorite lures and will most effectively use these when fishing difficult situations. Each lure has a specific purpose and can be selected according to its particular effectiveness.

By analogy, we might liken the tackle box and assorted lures to our personal testimonies. Those intimate, life-changing experiences and memories help equip us to share with others the personal relationship that we enjoy with the Lord. Just as good bait attracts a fish, so we can attract unbelievers to the Lord by our vibrant testimonies. Each day brings new opportunities for the Lord to do His miracles and to build memories in our lives that will encourage us and others in our spiritual journeys. Life's experiences provide all of us unique snapshots that can be shared with others. Truly there is power in a vibrant testimony (Rev. 12:11).

Perhaps you had a near-death experience, or financial disappointment, or a marital challenge or another story from your life that is similar to the person you are trying to disciple. Your story is a connecting point to the person's soul and memory. You can use your story to build a spiritual bridge to God's Word and yourself.

THE LAST CAST

Upon Christ's resurrection and appearance to the eleven disciples, He issued the Great Commission to them along the same shoreline where He first met them. Once again we dip into this well of truth by visiting our theme verse, "All authority has been given to Me in heaven and on earth. Go therefore and make disciples of all the nations, baptizing them in the name of the Father and of the Son and of the Holy Spirit, teaching them to observe all things that I have commanded you; and lo, I am with you always, even to the end of the age" (Matt. 28:18–20).

I am sure that most Christians have heard or read the Great Commission many times. Yet it is surprising how many of them are still standing on the shore, watching others fish for souls. Perhaps some feel their equipment is not good enough? Have we forgotten who issues the equipment? Many believe this work should be left to the real pros: pastors, priests, missionaries, and church workers. But the Great Commission was written to all Christians.

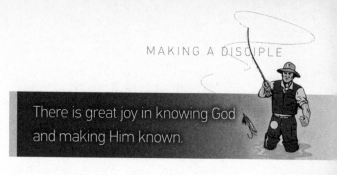

There is great joy in knowing God and making Him known.

Jesus said, "Now he who received seed among the thorns is he who hears the word, and the cares of this world and the deceitfulness of riches choke the word, and he becomes unfruitful" (Matt. 13:22). Let us not get choked out because we fail to be doers of the word. If we are going to be doers of the Word, we must participate in fulfilling the Great Commission. Of course, there are some who feel that the fish might not be interested. We look at the way our culture is going and give up on the fight. However, God promises that His Word will not return void (Isa. 55:10–11). A spiritual mentor who is serious about his call realizes that there is a spiritual vacuum in each person—an empty spirit crying out for God. Saint Augustine once said, "Our hearts are restless until they rest in Thee."[2]

People are seeking meaning and purpose in life. The reality is that the fish are very hungry. Our concern, then, is more a question of how we present the Word in a way they can understand and when we should do so. In his book *Jesus Christ, Disciple Maker*, Bill Hull suggested: "When Jesus calls a person, he calls him or her to a purpose, a dream, a goal, a life-changing vision. The vision is to be a fisher of men. These Galilean men [the disciples] understood fishing, and they were certainly acquainted with the lost state of men. Therefore, the call to fish for men turned their heads; their hearts were aflame with the idea!"[3]

When you stop and think about it, there are people you see every day who will never see Jesus in anyone but you. They may have never entered a church, gone to a Bible study, or watched an evangelistic television program. That is why we need to understand the importance of using our gifts and our talents to be fishers of men. *It's time to go fishing!*

BIBLE STUDY

> But sanctify the Lord God in your hearts, and always be ready to give a defense to everyone who asks you a reason for the hope that is in you, with meekness and fear. (1 Peter 3:15)

☐ What does it mean to "sanctify [set apart] the Lord God in your hearts"? How is this done? Why is it vitally important for a discipler or mentor?

☐ If someone asked you to explain why you seem so hopeful of the future, how would you answer? What *is* your hope for the future?

☐ Why does Peter command us to share our testimony "with meekness and fear"? Why is meekness important when discussing what God has done for you? What is the "fear" that Peter has in mind here?

LOST IN THE
FOG OF LIFE

For God has not given us a spirit of
fear, but of power and of love and of a
sound mind.

—2 Timothy 1:7

Most of us have been lost at one time or another. If you are an outdoorsman, I can almost guarantee that you have been lost. One past experience I had looms in my mind as a time when I wish I had Jesus in person in my boat.

It was a cold December morning in the San Francisco Bay area. The weather forecast indicated that there was a chance of showers with heavy fog in the inland areas. My fishing buddy Rick and I headed east toward the Sacramento River delta, not paying much attention to road conditions. It's typically foggy over the pass at this time of year, although it's not often dense. As we arrived at the marina, I commented to Rick that it was going to be a challenge to see many birds diving for baitfish with the heavy fog conditions. I noticed that the marina parking lot was empty—and that should have told me something.

Climbing aboard, we launched the boat into the heavy mist. I could tell that Rick was feeling very uneasy about motoring off into this strange environment. But I reassured him that all was fine. After all, he was with one of the top fishermen in California and a man who knew the delta well.

It was important to motor along at idling speed, since we could not see beyond the front of the boat. We used the dark shadows of the old sunken barges on the starboard side as a reference point. If we just followed this line of sunken barges, we would soon come to my favorite slough (waterway). We were out for about fifteen minutes when we came to the last barge. All we had to do was cross the slough in front of us, and waiting on the rocky far bank would be five-pound black bass and several of their striped bass cousins. I had caught and released some of them just a few days earlier.

The biting cold and the endless fog seemed to worsen as we moved across the slough. I needed to correct our steering to the right if we were going to run a correct course, as my boat tended to pull to the left when motoring at low speeds. We had been totally quiet for about five minutes. Finally, Rick broke the silence and asked, "When will we get there?" He was obviously getting anxious. I tried to reassure him. Deep down, though, I knew something was wrong. I had miscalculated the mark. Perhaps I had overcorrected the steering. I guess I was too proud to stop and admit my confusion.

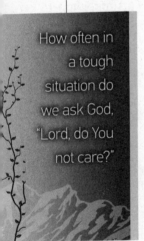

How often in a tough situation do we ask God, "Lord, do You not care?"

After ten minutes of fruitless efforts, however, I had thoroughly convinced both of us that I had no idea where we were. The river current was running quickly, and I visualized my new Ranger bass boat drifting under the Golden Gate Bridge and out to sea without anyone noticing. What a ridiculous situation we found ourselves in.

With Jesus in our boat, we don't have to experience the storm alone.

I turned off the engine and stared into the fog. Why on earth had I left the marina, let alone my nice warm bed? Rick's stress level was building with every passing moment. The idea of going fishing had been to get his mind off such things as death, tension, and himself—and to redirect his negative thinking. Our present situation was not helping matters. We drifted for what seemed like hours, although it was only fifteen to twenty minutes. If that weren't bad enough, a noise began to emerge from the fog. Terror began to grip my heart as I realized it was the sound of the propeller wash of a very large ship.

Russian ships regularly enter San Francisco Bay and move up the Sacramento River to the San Joaquin River in Stockton, where they load their empty hulls with grain from several riverside locations. As this ship steamed up the river with its radar on, I knew they were hoping not to hit any obstructions. Why the skipper hadn't picked a clear day to move upriver puzzled me.

We were sitting somewhere near this approaching ship in a relatively small fiberglass boat that seldom shows up on radar. *Is it headed in our direction? Should we move? What direction?* We decided to stay where we were and pray. The ship passed on our port side, probably 150 feet away. We heard every beat of the prop blades hitting the water. It was close enough that the wake nearly capsized my boat. It was a close call we would remember for life.

As I gathered my senses and realized that God had again spared my life, I began to pray. God reminded me that the solutions to my problem were already in my boat. The fog horn in the distance that I was hearing reminded me that God's voice spoke to me in prayer and meditation. The map in the glove box was what would direct me to a safe refuge. God's Word is our map to peace and an eternal relationship with the living God. The compass on my dashboard would guide us to the true north, just as the Holy Spirit guides us to the true God. And Rick represented the Christian fellowship that is needed to help us through those tough times.

As I thought about this brush with tragedy, I was reminded of how often Jesus' disciples became sidetracked, discouraged, frightened, and even lost. Their priorities were tested regularly. Even Jesus challenged the disciples' personal growth and development as spiritual leaders when He asked them, "Why are you fearful, O you of little faith?" (Matt. 8:26). Wasn't He really asking them, "Why don't you have your spiritual priorities in better order?" Jesus knew they needed to mature in their faith, yet He remained sensitive to their frustrations and confusion. To help them better define their priorities, He offered them a simple but profound message—to follow and trust Him.

THE GIFT OF FAITH

Jesus taught His disciples that He would give them a precious gift, one that would help them the rest of their lives. This gift was something they needed in order to defeat the enemy and establish His church: faith.

The strengthening of faith for the disciples would come in a variety of ways. On two occasions, Jesus met the disciples where they felt most comfortable, fishing on the Sea of Galilee. These experienced fishermen were confident in their skills and knowledge of the way this lake behaved. But on two occasions, they experienced something that caused them to be afraid that they would drown (Matt. 14; Mark 4). As He did with me in the San Francisco Bay, Jesus needed to tear down the disciples' self-reliance and have them become men of faith and trust. Let's remember the account in Mark 4 as our example for building faith.

> On the same day, when evening had come, He said to them, "Let us cross over to the other side." Now when they had left the multitude, they took Him along in the boat as He was. And other little boats were also with Him. And a great windstorm arose, and the waves beat into the boat, so that it was already filling. But He was in the stern, asleep on a pillow. And they awoke Him and said to Him, "Teacher, do You not care that we are perishing?" Then He arose and rebuked the wind, and said to the sea, "Peace, be still!" And the wind ceased and there was a great calm. But He said to them, "Why are you so fearful? How is it that you have no faith?" And they feared exceedingly, and said to one another, "Who can this be, that even the wind and the sea obey Him!" (vv. 35–41)

First, the disciples did not listen to (or did not believe) what Jesus said: "Let us cross over to the other side." They got caught up in the present (albeit difficult) situation and could only see the wind and the water and the high waves.

Next, they questioned His care for them. How often in a tough situation do we ask God, "Lord, do You not care?" Like the disciples, we often look to our own resources to resolve the problems we are experiencing, forgetting the One who is in our boat: Jesus. We think of ways to battle the storms in our lives and then when we are at wit's end we drop to our knees, asking Him to help us. With Jesus in our boat we don't have to experience the storm alone. With Jesus in our boat we have a Comforter who will help us work through the trials and tribulations that life brings to each of us. As I found out in the San Francisco Bay, the Holy Spirit, God's Word, prayer, and the fellowship of other believers are within our reach. All we have to do is use them.

WHY DO STORMS COME OUR WAY?

Sometimes God allows storms to come our way so that our relationship with Him will be strengthened. There are occasions when God even sends a storm into our lives to adjust our thinking and direction. His plan for our lives is always greater than anything we could imagine. When we are off course and moving in the direction that could produce dire consequences, God may deliver a tempest that draws us back to Him.

Maybe we only put Jesus in our boat for Sunday church. But He earnestly wants us to have fellowship with Him daily. Jesus is a gentleman, however, not a pirate. He doesn't jump into our boat without being asked. He wants to direct and guide us, but only when we are willing to give control of our lives to Him who is able to foresee the consequences of our decisions and behavior. When I finally came to my senses in the San Francisco Bay, I realized that the resources needed to get me out of the fog were within reach. I just needed to use them. If I hadn't opened the compartment in my boat to get the map and compass out, I might not be writing this book today.

There are storms in our lives that come upon us because we have chosen to be disobedient. In such situations the issues we face are self-created, and the consequences of our sin create problems with how life is being lived out. Our sin can create chaos that causes our lives to spin out of control, much like being caught in a hurricane. When we are disobedient to God, we are basically leaving Him ashore in our thinking and actions; therefore, the result of our defiance is living in separation from God. Our God is a jealous God and desires us to be in relationship with Him.

The Devil prowls around our lives seeking whom he can devour and trip up. Scripture warns us to be alert and attentive to the Devil's ploys: "Be disciplined and stay on guard. Your enemy the devil is prowling around outside like a roaring lion, just waiting *and hoping for the chance* to devour someone. Resist him and be strong in your faith, knowing that your brothers and sisters throughout the world are fellow sufferers with you. After you have suffered for a little while, the God of grace who has called you [to His everlasting presence] through Jesus the Anointed will restore you, support you, strengthen you, and ground you" (1 Peter 5:8–10 The Voice).

> Jesus is a gentleman, not a pirate. He doesn't jump into our boat without being asked.

If you have ever heard a lion roar, you have some idea why he is called the "king of the jungle." It is a frightening sound that can be heard over long distances and calls you to immediate attention. And the goal of the lion on the hunt is to rip you into pieces, to render you helpless, and to kill you. A lion on the hunt is not a tame nor a gentle creature; he is cunning, vicious, deadly, and without mercy. This is the picture that Peter is drawing of Satan, the enemy of our souls who seeks to tear our lives apart.

Perhaps the most obvious storm that stirs the sea of life is recognizing we live in a fallen world. Adam broke fellowship with God when he chose to disobey Him, and today we experience suffering and trouble just because we are part of this fallen world. A world that has turned its back on God is a world awaiting judgment. Unfortunately, many of the issues America is facing today are a result of God's judgment upon the land and its people due to distancing ourselves from the godly principles that this nation was founded upon. The book of Daniel, John's Revelation, and the Gospels are filled with prophecies that have become reality in the storms and lions that we face today.

Jesus wants His disciples and spiritual mentors to be prepared for those storms. He has told us that He is the rock.

> Therefore whoever hears these sayings of Mine, and does them, I will liken him to a wise man who built his house on the rock: and the rain descended, the floods came, and the winds blew and beat on that house; and it did not fall, for it was founded on the rock. But everyone who hears these sayings of Mine, and does not do them, will be like a foolish man who built his house on the sand: and the rain descended, the floods came, and the winds blew and beat on that house; and it fell. And great was its fall. (Matt. 7:24–27)

Note that Jesus didn't say *if* the storms come. No, He said that storms *will* come. As James, the half brother of Jesus, also testified, "My brethren, count it all joy when you fall into various trials" (James 1:2). The house that Jesus spoke of in the parable about the rock refers to our marriages, our families, our churches, even our country. If we are to be the disciples He wants us to be, we must weather the storms of life either by having Jesus in our boats or by standing with Him on the rock. Either way,

He desires to stand with us. All we have to do is invite Him to be with us.

It's interesting to think about how we react when the storms of life hit us. Jesus asks us to do the opposite of what most of us want to do in the flesh. In the flesh, we want to run away from the storm, tuck into a fetal position, and pretend it's not happening, or give in to the raging fingers of the storm that grip our hearts and minds. Jesus never said that we would not be afraid at times, but Paul said "God has not given us a spirit of fear, but of power and of love and of a sound mind" (2 Tim. 1:7). If we let it, fear has a way of grabbing our throats and strangling the life out of us. God's Word will guide us toward the right attitude when facing challenges: "Therefore we also, since we are surrounded by so great a cloud of witnesses, let us lay aside every weight, and the sin which so easily ensnares us, and let us run with endurance the race that is set before us, looking unto Jesus, the author and finisher of our faith, who for the joy that was set before Him endured the cross, despising the shame, and has sat down at the right hand of the throne of God" (Heb. 12:1–2).

CHALLENGES DEVELOP FAITH AND CHARACTER

In an earlier chapter we looked at Scripture passages commanding men not to be afraid, and we considered the fact that we are called to be courageous. At the same time, the challenges God sends our way—those very things we might be tempted to fear— can actually develop both faith and character in our lives.

Let me illustrate this with a fish story. As easterners transplanted themselves to the West Coast, they found themselves

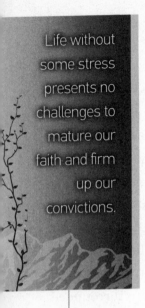

Life without some stress presents no challenges to mature our faith and firm up our convictions.

longing for the East Coast cod. It was often shipped by rail to several fine-dining restaurants on the West Coast. The customers, though, complained that the fish just weren't the same. Despite providing aerated containers with water from the original source, the fish arrived soft and tasteless.

Then someone reckoned that the fish needed to be challenged in a real-life environment. Catfish and bullheads were among the natural predators of the cods, and they were introduced into the shipping containers—and codfish traveled across the country in close company with their mortal enemies. Interestingly, from that time forward the fish arrived firm and tasty.

Life without some stress presents no challenges to mature our faith and firm up our convictions. Real living involves dealing with the catfish of life. It is healthy for us to encounter people and circumstances who challenge us and refine our character. Through these challenges we are able to test our faith and witness God's miracles. The raging waters of our lives will be calmed as we rest in God's sovereign hands. If we focus on the Lord and His promises, we will not be robbed of joy in our lives, despite the circumstances. Popular pastor and author Chuck Swindoll tells us that worry, stress, and fear can be joy stealers. Listen to his words:

> Worry is an inordinate anxiety about something that may or may not occur. It has been my observation that what is being worried about usually does not occur. But worry eats away at joy like slow-working acid while we are waiting for the outcome. . . .

Stress is a little more acute than worry. Stress is intense strain over a situation we cannot change or control—something beyond our control. . . . And instead of releasing it to God, we churn over it. It is in that restless churning stage that our stress is intensified. Usually the thing that plagues us is not as severe as we make it out to be.

Fear, on the other hand, is different from worry and stress. It is dreadful uneasiness over the presence of danger, evil, or pain. As with the other two, however, fear usually makes things appear worse than they really are.[1]

We need to keep things in perspective. If we focus on our fears, threats always appear bigger and worse than they really are. But if we focus on God's sovereign control, fear is kept in check and God uses our experiences to mature our faith.

FAITH DISPELS FEAR

Faith can dispel fear, but only in proportion to its strength. As the faith of the disciples grew, their strength to overcome their fears also increased. We need to relax in the promises Christ gave His first-century disciples. During His farewell discourse prior to His betrayal, Jesus comforted His disciples by saying, "Don't get lost in despair; believe in God, and keep on believing in Me" (John 14:1 The Voice). Moreover, Jesus said, "My peace is the legacy I leave to you. I don't give gifts like those of this world. Do not let your heart be troubled or fearful" (v. 27 The Voice).

The disciples' belief in these wonderful promises allowed them to mature in their faith. They were able to declare their assurance in Christ and victory over fear in their ministries.

Following are some verses that are especially helpful for those confronting fear:

> For God has not given us a spirit of fear, but of power and of love and of a sound mind. (2 Tim. 1:7)

> So we may boldly say: "The LORD is my helper; I will not fear. What can man do to me?" (Heb. 13:6)

> For you did not receive the spirit of bondage again to fear, but you received the Spirit of adoption by whom we cry out, "Abba, Father." (Rom. 8:15)

> There is no fear in love; but perfect love casts out fear, because fear involves torment. But he who fears has not been made perfect in love. (1 John 4:18)

It is important for us to remember that a disciple is not without hope. God uses the challenges in our lives as opportunities to grow us into the likeness of Jesus. Remember the One who is in your boat. The psalmist wrote in Psalm 56:3, "Whenever I am afraid, I will trust in You." Because fear will come upon us so quickly, it is difficult not to have a knee-jerk reaction and depend on ourselves to solve a situation and reduce the "afraid factor." This is the time when we must work on being calm, check out our God-given resources, and then react. Of course, the more time we spend in prayer, Bible study, scripture memory, and fellowship with other Christians, the more we will turn to Christ and His abundant resources when we are afraid.

BIBLE STUDY

For God has not given us a spirit of fear, but of power and of love and of a sound mind. (2 Tim. 1:7)

☐ What characteristics of the Holy Spirit does Paul touch on in this verse? How can these characteristics help you to overcome fear?

☐ What is the "sound mind" referred to here? Why is it important to have sound thinking when doing battle against fear?

☐ What are three fears that try to rob you of a joyful life (Ps. 20:1–7; Jer. 9:23; 1 Cor. 5:2; 1 Tim. 6:17)?

MEETING
TOGETHER

> The church by definition is the
> greatest gathering of potential ser-
> vants in the world, but she is also the
> most notorious vehicle for disappoint-
> ing, discouraging, and even destroying
> them.
>
> **—Sue Mallory, *The Equipping Church*[1]**

The first Special Forces units had their start in World War II, but they gained popularity and attention in a speech given by President John F. Kennedy on May 25, 1961, when he announced his intention to allocate over $100 million to strengthen US special operations forces and expand American capabilities in unconventional warfare.

This was the beginning of the Navy SEALs as we know them today. Many Americans first became aware of the capabilities of the SEALs when an article broke about the invasion of Grenada in October 1983. Both SEAL Team 4 and SEAL Team 6 partic-ipated in the US invasion of Grenada. The SEALs' two primary missions were the extraction of Grenada's governor-general and the capture of Grenada's only radio tower. Neither mission was well briefed or sufficiently supported with timely intelligence, and the SEALs ran into trouble from the very beginning. One of their two transport planes missed its drop zone, and four SEALs drowned in a rain squall while making an airborne insertion with their boats off the island's coast. Their bodies were never recovered.

After regrouping from their initial insertion into Grenada, the SEALs split into two teams and proceeded to their objectives. After digging in at the governor's mansion, the SEALs realized they had forgotten to load the cryptographic codes in their satellite radios. As Grenadian and Cuban troops surrounded the team, the SEALs' only radio ran out of battery power, and they used the landline telephone in the governor's mansion to call in AC-130 fire support. The SEALs were pinned down in the mansion overnight and were relieved and extracted by a group of marines the following morning.

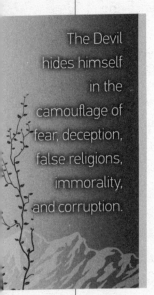

The Devil hides himself in the camouflage of fear, deception, false religions, immorality, and corruption.

The team sent to the radio station also ran into communication problems. As soon as the SEALs reached the radio facility, they found themselves unable to raise their command post. After beating back several waves of Grenadian and Cuban troops supported by BTR-60s (Russian wheeled amphibious armored vehicles), the SEALs decided that their position at the radio tower was untenable. They destroyed the station and fought their way to the water, where they hid from patrolling enemy forces. After the enemy had given up their search, the SEALs, some wounded, swam into the open sea where they were extracted several hours later after being spotted by a reconnaissance plane.[2]

What held these men together during such a trying time? How were they able to keep on fighting despite the overwhelming odds against them? These men had many wonderful attributes, including being well-trained, disciplined, courageous, and fit, while also having good leadership, a willingness to sacrifice, a plan and vision to free those who were captive, and a willing obedience to commands. They had studied and were prepared to engage the enemy.

The battle that most disciples face today is, in many ways, not much different than what those SEALs faced on the beaches and mountaintops in Grenada. The Devil hides himself in the camouflage of fear, deception, false religions, immorality, and corruption. He is as sneaky as a snake slithering in the wet grass, as deadly as a roaring lion hunting his prey, as cunning as a wolf in sheep's clothing, as deadly as a vampire bat, and as crafty as a serpent.

THE WELL-TRAINED DISCIPLE

Our opening story about the brave men on the SEAL teams that invaded Grenada demonstrates the courage, conviction, and dedication needed to be an effective disciple. When you think about it, the attributes associated with being an effective spiritual mentor are similar to those found in a good soldier:

Well-trained: As we see in Exodus 17:10, Joshua led the battle, and his field training would also serve him well later in Canaan. God had trained Moses for his work, and Moses in turn trained Joshua. This is the pattern the Lord wants His people to follow today as well. He wants us to train other believers to succeed us, to share the wisdom that He has given us during our walk with Him, and to encourage younger men to walk in faith. The reality is that we need more warriors for Jesus; God taught Moses that the battle is won by faith, and Moses passed that lesson on to Joshua. A spiritual mentor will train others in this important lesson.

Disciplined: The SEALs needed to have strong self-discipline to enable them to face the unexpected and devise new strategies on the spot, without falling into panic and chaos. As spiritual mentors, we are to be self-disciplined through the conviction of the Holy Spirit in our lives. Paul warns us that the flesh is in constant war against the Spirit, and the follower of Christ must be constantly striving to put to death the desires of the flesh. He wrote, "So, my brothers and sisters, you owe the flesh nothing! You do not need to live according to its ways, *so abandon its oppressive regime.* For if your life is just about satisfying the impulses of your sinful nature, then prepare to die. But if you have invited the Spirit to destroy these selfish desires, you will experience life. If the Spirit of God is leading you, then *take comfort in knowing* you are His children" (Rom. 8:12–14 The Voice). Scripture further reminds us, "You have not yet resisted to bloodshed, striving against sin. And you have forgotten the exhortation which speaks to you as to sons: 'My son, do not despise the chastening of the LORD, nor be discouraged when you are rebuked by Him; for whom the LORD loves He chastens, and scourges every son whom He receives" (Heb. 12:4–6).

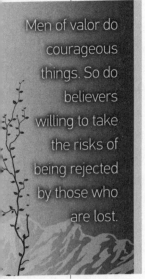

Men of valor do courageous things. So do believers willing to take the risks of being rejected by those who are lost.

Courageous: Men of valor do courageous things. So do believers willing to take the risks of being rejected by those who are lost. In previous chapters

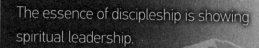

The essence of discipleship is showing spiritual leadership.

we have discussed the fact that fear is our enemy, and the courageous man is the one who feels fear and continues to move forward in disregard of that fear. The spiritual mentor will experience the emotion of fear, but he will override it by continuing to obey God through faith. "Be strong and of good courage, do not fear nor be afraid of them; for the LORD your God, He is the One who goes with you. He will not leave you nor forsake you" (Deut. 31:6).

Fitness: Being fit involves more than being in good shape and physically strong. It's about having a balanced lifestyle, including prayer, meditation, Bible study, physical exercise, nutritional food, and plenty of sleep. Scripture suggests that fitness involves putting into action, performing, or taking pain. Disciples will take pain and need to know how to handle it. Often the pain comes from mental stress, heartache, discouragement, or broken relationships. The spiritual mentor will exhibit spiritual fitness in his own life, and he will strive to teach its importance to those he mentors. As Paul reminds us, "Reject worldly fables. Refuse old wives' tales. Instead, train yourself toward godliness. Although training your body has certain payoffs, godliness benefits all things—holding promise for life here and now and promise for the life that is coming" (1 Tim. 4:7–8 The Voice).

Leadership: The essence of discipleship is showing spiritual leadership. In the previous chapter we discussed the role of an intentional spiritual mentor. Every small group needs leadership. The concept of "leaderless groups" is not valid. This does not mean that groups need only one dominant leader, but rather that a good group needs good leadership, whether from one or from all. First Timothy and Titus are full of ideas for being an intentional leader.

In 1 Timothy 3 we find some of the criteria for being a spiritual leader and overseer. Paul's admonition to the younger Timothy reminds him that being in leadership is a "noble task." It requires discipline, obedience to God's Word, and a gentle, loving spirit. In his closing instruction to Timothy (1 Tim. 6:11–12), Paul summed up his challenge in the most eloquent way: "But you, O man of God, flee these things and pursue righteousness, godliness, faith, love, patience, gentleness. Fight the good fight of faith."

Sacrifice: Four of the brave SEALs gave their lives swimming ashore into a hostile environment to help save others. Similarly, a spiritual mentor might well be called upon to make some self-sacrifice for those he mentors. A person committed to discipling will often give up personal desires in order to make time to pray, prepare, and fellowship with those disciples under his care. It is through that sacrifice that others are eternally saved. In Genesis 22 we find Abraham willing to obey God with the ultimate sacrifice—that of his son.

Plan: The SEALs in our opening story had a plan, but when they arrived in Grenada things went disastrously wrong. The problems were that their plan was ill-informed, based upon faulty intelligence, and poorly communicated to those involved. And here we come back to the word *intentional:* without having a plan, discipleship ends up being at best a hit-or-miss proposition. Most of the people I've talked to who failed at discipleship had not planned or taken advantage of a purposeful program that was bathed in Scripture and prayer. Our mentoring plans must be founded upon God's Word and fortified by prayer, and they must also be clearly communicated to those whom we disciple. Jesus warned of the importance of planning when He told His followers to count the cost of discipleship: "For which of you, intending to build a tower, does not sit down first and count the cost, whether he has enough to finish it?" (Luke 14:28).

Obedience: Despite their initial losses due to poor intelligence from Washington, the SEALs rallied around good on-the-ground commanders who issued instructions that ultimately saved their lives and the lives of many noncombatants. Our Supreme Commander is God, and His intelligence is never wrong. He tells disciples if we are obedient to His commands, it will be well with us. It's not faith plus obedience that equals salvation; it is obedient faith that equals salvation. Spiritual mentors have seen the evidence that true faith is verified in one's obedience to God. Faith that excludes obedience won't save anyone. This important point is addressed in James 2: "Thus also faith by itself, if it does not have works [obedience], is dead" (v. 17).

Christ asked us to build our lives in obedience to His Word. When we are young Christians, we don't see the direct connection between faith and obedience. As we immerse ourselves in His Word, we begin to see more clearly the obedient life. "But now made manifest, and by the prophetic Scriptures made known to all nations, according to the commandment of the everlasting God, for obedience to the faith—to God, alone wise, be glory through Jesus Christ forever. Amen" (Rom. 16:26–27).

Prepare for the battle: The Navy SEALs are arguably the best-trained and most equipped soldiers in the world. They perform at the highest level and utilize their training, skills, abilities, and equipment to carry out their mission, always prepared to do battle with the enemy. Our greatest enemy is Satan. Our mission is to influence others to know God and make Him known before Satan can dig his claws into their hearts. His influences are destroying thousands of people every day.

> The most effective spiritual mentors are people who serve in churches that have developed supportive small group ministries.

In writing to the people in Ephesus, the apostle Paul tells us that the spiritual battles we face are even more difficult than the physical assaults that soldiers deal with. He tells us to put on the whole armor of God, that we might be able to stand against the Devil (Eph. 6:11–17). We are to put on the belt of truth, the breastplate of righteousness, the shoes of preparation, the shield of faith, and the helmet of salvation, and to pick up the sword of the Spirit and the lances of prayer. Like a good soldier we are to make every effort to prepare ourselves for battle. "So it shall be, when you are on the verge of battle, that the priest shall approach and speak to the people. And he shall say to them, 'Hear, O Israel: Today you are on the verge of battle with your enemies. Do not let your heart faint, do not be afraid, and do not tremble or be terrified because of them; for the LORD your God is He who goes with you, to fight for you against your enemies, to save you'" (Deut. 20:2–4).

STRENGTH IN NUMBERS

Just as a small group of elite fighting men can be more effective than an entire division of soldiers, so too can a small group of men be very valuable in soul-winning. As mentioned previously, ministry is not done in a vacuum. We need the encouragement, accountability, spiritual gifting, and support of others to be most effective.

The most effective spiritual mentors are people who serve in churches that have developed supportive small group ministries. Real relationships cannot be built from a distance or in isolation or in a crowded church, or even through social media. Relationship with others is God's way to hone our motivation, attitudes, and theology. It is with others that we apply God's truth. A relational environment is where friends and strangers can gather to work through real-life problems and share our goal of becoming a discipleship family and network. When churches appropriate the hidden talent sitting on the pews and get them into small groups, they will see people mature from the infant Christian (who usually is a taker) to a mature adult Christian (who is a reproducer and a giver).

The apostle Paul, writing to his disciple Timothy, talked about the importance of trusting in reliable and faith-filled men for personal growth: "You therefore, my son, be strong in the grace that is in Christ Jesus. And the things that you have heard from me among many witnesses, commit these to faithful men who will be able to teach others also. You therefore must endure hardship as a good soldier of Jesus Christ" (2 Tim. 2:1–3). Just like our Navy SEALs in the battle for Grenada, we are strong in our faith because of faithful and dedicated men who share and support our ideals and focus of Jesus Christ.

There is tremendous potential power in a small group ministry of eight to twelve committed spiritual mentors camped around the Word of God with a vision to reach their community for Jesus. A dynamic church will have several groups of men that will be part of the fabric of the church body. Some groups will be theme driven, others will be general groups, and some might even be directed in specific areas (e.g., discipleship training, service, hospitality, security, teaching Sunday school, pastoral support, event planning, workshop and retreat development, and various sports affinity groups).

THE TWELVE AS A SMALL GROUP

Jesus could have picked many ways to announce the good news that the Son of God came to bring God to all people and all people to one another. The gathering of the Twelve is foundational to the proclamation and demonstration of the gospel as good news: God is with us; God has come to earth to show us the way of salvation (John 1:1).

The purpose of the first small group was to train and equip apostles (those who are sent forth) for the purpose of spreading the good news throughout the world. Jesus first called the small group to come and follow, then to go and minister. As the disciples learned from Jesus, this inner group of twelve grew out of discipleship training into deploying as apostles. Training, equipping, and learning are involved in the discipleship process, so that we are better prepared to serve as a spiritual mentor and to accomplish the mission that God has put before us—and mission should always be the fulfillment of learning. The vision and plan for discipleship was focused and launched in the group experience and ministry of the Twelve. They saw discipleship modeled by Christ and had an opportunity to try it themselves under His guidance.

SMALL GROUPS IN TODAY'S CHURCH

In his masterful work titled *The Big Book on Small Groups*, Jeffery Arnold wrote:

> The answer to this complex problem may appear overly simple, but small groups can go a long way toward engaging people in personal growth. Small groups help them to grow in relationships and stimulate them to make a difference in their families, church and world. Once formed into small family-like groups of partners-in-discipleship, people begin to know themselves and others better. They move past surface conversation and the preliminary fears of opening themselves up to others, and they begin to experience real fellowship. While weekly worship services and a 'fellowship hour' afterwards are undeniably important, they alone cannot provide the depth that is necessary for believers to take root and grow.[3]

HOW TO BEGIN A SMALL GROUP

The traits we find in the people developing a small group are much the same as described earlier in this chapter about being a good soldier. With prayer and the blessing of your pastor, an individual or group of individuals needs to determine the purpose and intent of the group. A good question to ask others is,

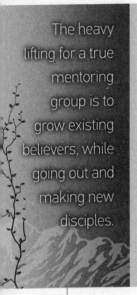

The heavy lifting for a true mentoring group is to grow existing believers, while going out and making new disciples.

"What personal and spiritual needs do you and your friends at church have that could be met within a small group?"

A decision should be made on how many people would be in the group—ideally eight to twelve. Individuals who share the same interests in the vision should be given a personal invitation to try the group for a couple of meetings. As the group moves forward, and sharing and sharpening occurs (Prov. 27:17), feedback should be encouraged so that the group can discover the issues that are impacting the men. For most young Christians, try to keep the topical discussion to six to eight meetings, then regroup and evaluate your next area of interest. As the group matures, more time should be given to drilling down into deeper biblical truths that transform lives. One of the goals for the group should include having a vision that ultimately spawns new groups. That is the process of reproduction.

Spiritual growth usually occurs as people have the opportunity to interact together in God's Word, drawing out personal applications so that each one matures in Christ. One part of your group's purpose will be to discover and meet needs within each other.[4] When caring friendships are formed, men begin to trust and unpack the stuff that was previously hidden.

The psychologists I have spoken with have discovered that many clients improve more rapidly in small group therapy than through individual counseling. The potential is great for body-life nurture and healing in small groups. Through a complete network of small groups involving all the church, a call could go out to the small group leaders whenever an emergency arises.

Then group members could assist the pastor(s) in situations like the death of a family member, a financial crisis, and so on. They could visit group members in the hospital, bring in meals for the sick, loan cars, help with child care, and pray specific prayers.

Earlier in this book, I quoted a statistic that, in the average church, only one to two baptisms occur per year. We need to be sure that our small groups don't end up as social clubs or good buddy fellowships. The heavy lifting for a true mentoring group is to grow existing believers, while going out and making new disciples. If we don't have this as a goal, we could end up like a club in the story below.

FISHLESS FISHERMEN

There was a group called Fishermen's Fellowship. They were surrounded by streams and lakes full of hungry fish. They met regularly to discuss the call to fish, the abundance of fish, and the thrill of catching fish. They got excited about fishing. Someone suggested that they needed a philosophy of fishing, so they carefully defined and redefined fishing strategies and tactics.

Then they realized that they had been going at it backward. They had approached fishing from the point of view of fishermen and not from the point of view of the fish. How do fish view the world? How does the fisherman appear to the fish? What do fish eat and when? These are all good things to know. So they began research studies and attended conferences on fishing. Some traveled to faraway places to study different kinds of fish with different habits. Some got PhDs in fishiology. But no one had yet gone fishing.

So a committee was formed to send out fishermen. As prospective fishing places outnumbered the fishermen, the committee needed to determine priorities. A priority list of fishing places was posted on bulletin boards in all the Fellowship Halls. Still no one was fishing. A survey was launched to find out why. Most did not answer the questionnaire, but from those who did respond it was discovered that some felt called to study fish, a few to furnish fishing equipment, and several to go around encouraging fishermen. What with meetings, conferences, and seminars, others simply didn't have time to fish.

Jake was a newcomer to the Fishermen's Fellowship. After one stirring meeting of the Fellowship, Jake went fishing. He tried a few things, got the hang of it, and caught a choice fish. At the next meeting, he told his story, was honored for his catch, and was then scheduled to speak at all the Fellowship chapters and tell how he did it.

Now because of all the speaking and his election to the board of directors of the Fishermen's Fellowship, Jake no longer had time to go fishing. Soon he began to feel restless and empty. He longed to feel the tug on the line once again. He cut the speaking, resigned from the board, and said to a friend, "Let's go fishing." They did—just the two of them—and they caught fish.

The members of the Fishermen's Fellowship were many, the fish were plentiful, but the numbers of those actually fishing were few.[5]

This book is written to the true Fishermen's Fellowship—the church—made up of disciples who use their God-given talents in the marketplace of life. Work environments, social contacts, academic institutions, and friendships are uniquely different for every believer, and there is a host of contacts awaiting each disciple-fisherman.

BIBLE STUDY

Let us consider how to inspire each other to greater love and to righteous deeds, not forgetting to gather as a community, as some have forgotten, but encouraging each other, especially as the day *of His return* approaches. (Heb. 10:24–25 The Voice)

How faithful are you in supporting the mission of your church? Where are you involved in your church and how are you making a difference?

Again, if two lie down together, they will keep warm; but how can one be warm alone? Though one may be overpowered by another, two can withstand him. And a threefold cord is not quickly broken. (Eccl. 4:11–12)

How do these verses apply to your life and ministry?

How can you help this concept be evident in your small group?

A PERSONAL MESSAGE

I have been privileged to be involved in helping to develop ministry to men's programs and resources for over thirty-two years. Discipleship and mentoring are not only the core of our faith, but the foundation of our ministry.

Men's Ministry Catalyst (a.k.a. Let's Go Fishing Ministry and Outdoor Connection Ministry) is one of the oldest men's ministries in the country. We seek to help churches pray, plan, and execute an effective ministry to men that intentionally transforms them into the likeness of Christ. With your support and God's enabling power, we can make a real difference in the lives of thousands with consulting, best practices, training, special kid's day programs, and regional men's events.

Men's Ministry Catalyst (MMC) has been a resource organization for churches and national ministries wishing to impact their communities with relevant messages and memory-building experiences. Most recently we have embarked upon a unique and exciting vision to develop state-of-the-art multimedia presentations to assist others in developing dynamic programs on various sport and ministry themes.

These presentations are accessible through the Internet and will provide testimonials and technique presentations from some of the top Christian football players, hunters, fishermen, archers, and outdoorsmen in the world. Our detailed format of program development and implementation will assist even the smallest fellowship in presenting a "world-class" program. These resources are ideal for church community outreach events, conference ministry, men's ministry programs, youth rallies, and pastors' retreats.

For more information on how you can access these resources, please contact: Dr. Jim Grassi, P.O. Box 3303 Post Falls, ID 83877 or through our website, www.mensministrycatalyst.org.

ABOUT THE AUTHOR

Dr. Jim Grassi is an award-winning author, communicator, outdoorsman, pastor, and former television co-host. He has presented hundreds of messages and programs around the world that helped equip people to fulfill the Great Commission (Matt. 28). He brings a sense of challenge, wisdom, excitement, and humor to his presentations as he connects with people of various cultures and backgrounds. Through his multimedia outreach ministry he encourages participants toward a greater understanding and appreciation of evangelism, discipleship, and the development of creating vibrant men's ministries. His practical approach to teaching biblical truth has captivated audiences around the world.

Jim Grassi is the founder/president of the culturally strategic Men's Ministry Catalyst, an organization he incorporated in 1981. Grassi is a recognized author of several books, including *The Ultimate Fishing Challenge, Heaven on Earth, In Pursuit of the Prize, The Ultimate Hunt, Wading Through the Chaos, Crunch Time, A Study Guide of Israel, The Ultimate Men's Ministry Encyclopedia, Crunch Time in the Red Zone, Gut's, Grace, and Glory—A Football Devotional,* and *Building a Ministry of Spiritual Mentoring.* Jim has also written numerous magazine articles, booklets, and tracts.

Grassi was born and reared in the San Francisco Bay area. Known for his evangelistic heart, he teaches people from a background of an outdoorsman, public administrator, hall of fame fisherman, college professor, businessman, community leader, and pastor. He has served as chaplain with the San Francisco 49ers, the Oakland Raiders, Hurricane Katrina, and the Post

Falls Idaho Police Department. His life experiences, study of discipleship, and work with hundreds of churches have given him a unique perspective on helping men to know God and make Him known.

GOD'S GAME PLAN FOR LIFE

Like a head coach developing a good game plan for the Super Bowl, our heavenly Father developed a plan for our salvation. He initially hoped man would connect with Him through His great Creation; Adam and Eve thought they had a better idea. Then God utilized great patriarchs like Moses and Joshua to present His plan to His chosen people (the Jews), then great kings, priests, judges, and prophets, only to be saddened with the condition of man's prideful spirit and sin-filled heart. So how does our Great Coach, God Almighty, get our attention? He sends in the best signal caller and sacrifice of all time—Jesus Christ.

The Romans Road lays out the only game plan for salvation through a series of Bible verses from the book of Romans. These verses form an easy-to-follow explanation of the message of salvation.

The Romans Road clearly defines

1. who needs salvation,

2. why we need salvation,

3. how God provides salvation,

4. how we receive salvation, and

5. the results of salvation.

THE ROMANS ROAD OF SALVATION

 Everyone needs salvation because we have all sinned.

> As it is written: "There is none righteous, no, not one; there is none who understands; there is none who seeks after God. They have all turned aside; they have together become unprofitable; there is none who does good, no, not even one." . . . All have sinned and fall short of the glory of God. (Rom. 3:10–12, 23)

 The price (or consequence) of sin is death.

> For the wages of sin is death, but the gift of God is eternal life in Christ Jesus our Lord. (Rom. 6:23)

 Jesus Christ died for our sins. He paid the price for our death.

> But God demonstrates His own love toward us, in that while we were still sinners, Christ died for us. (Rom. 5:8)

 We receive salvation and eternal life through faith in Jesus Christ.

> That if you confess with your mouth the Lord Jesus and believe in your heart that God has raised Him from the dead, you will be saved. For with the heart one believes unto righteousness, and with the mouth confession is made unto salvation. . . . For, "whoever calls on the name of the Lord shall be saved." (Rom. 10:9–10, 13)

Salvation through Jesus Christ brings us into a relationship of peace with God.

> Therefore, having been justified by faith, we have peace with God through our Lord Jesus Christ. (Rom. 5:1)

> There is therefore now no condemnation to those who are in Christ Jesus. (Rom. 8:1)

> For I am persuaded that neither death nor life, nor angels nor principalities nor powers, nor things present nor things to come, nor height nor depth, nor any other created thing, shall be able to separate us from the love of God which is in Christ Jesus our Lord. (Rom. 8:38–39)

RESPONDING TO THE ROMANS ROAD

If you believe the scriptures in Romans lead to the path of truth, you can respond by receiving God's free gift of salvation today. Here's how:

 Admit you are a sinner.

 Understand that as a sinner, you deserve death.

 Believe Jesus Christ died on the cross to save you from sin and death. Believe that He conquered death itself when He rose from the grave.

 Repent by turning from your old life of sin to a new life in Christ.

Receive, through faith in Jesus Christ, His free gift of salvation.

ADDITIONAL RESOURCES

For additional resources or assistance, please e-mail Men's Ministry Catalyst at www.mensministrycatalyst.org.

ACKNOWLEDGMENTS

GREAT LEADERS DON'T JUST MAKE FOLLOWERS, THEY MAKE OTHER LEADERS

In speaking about gratitude the esteemed Reverend Willis P. King said, "Gratitude is from the same root word as 'grace,' which signifies the free and boundless mercy of God. Thanksgiving is from the same root as 'think,' so that to think is to thank." I'm extremely grateful to people who have been my spiritual mentors: Dr. Chuck Swindoll, Stan Smith, Daryl Kraft, and Pastor Jim Putman. Through their messages, writings, and personal counsel these men have spoken God's truth into my life that has formed many of the ideas I've expressed in this work.

This project could not have been possible without the constant love, support, and encouragement of my wonderful bride, Louise. Thank you for being my faithful partner. It is a real blessing to work together for God's kingdom.

I'm especially indebted to all my Men's Catalyst Ministry partners, supporters, board members, and Dr. Karen C. Johnson, who have faithfully served and contributed to my understanding of discipleship.

Finally, I commend and thank the very gifted staff at Thomas Nelson Publishers. Their amazing talents and enthusiasm have encouraged me to perfect and refine the concepts involved in this difficult work. I especially want to thank my good friends, publisher Frank Couch, and my editors Maleah Bell and Gregory Benoit for their insights and editing of this manuscript.

Thank you, Jesus!

"Grow in the grace and knowledge of our Lord."
2 Peter 3:18

NOTES

INTRODUCTION

1. "U.S. Congregational Life Survey – Key Findings," U.S. Congregations, October 29, 2003, www.uscongregations.org/key.htm.
2. UK Christian Handbook online, www.ukchristianhandbook.org.uk, June 2002.
3. Church for Men, www.churchformen.com/allmen.php, October 10, 2006.
4. Quoted in Sid Woodruff, "Tune to Men's Needs," Lifeway.com, http://www.lifeway.com/Article/Tune-to-Mens-Needs, accessed June 21, 2013.
5. Dietrich Bonhoeffer, *The Cost of Discipleship* (New York: Touchstone, 1959), 54.
6. George Barna, *Revolution* (Carol Stream, IL: Tyndale House Publishers, Inc., 2005), 8.
7. Ibid., 14.
8. "America's Families and Living Arrangements: 2012," U.S. Census Bureau, http://www.census.gov/hhes/families/data/cps2012.html, accessed June 21, 2013.

CHAPTER 1

1. Patrick Morley, *Pastoring Men* (Chicago, IL: Moody Publishers, 2009), 33; emphasis in original.
2. Kent Fillinger, "The Best Indicator of Church Growth: Baptisms in Church Planting," *Journey* magazine, April 10, 2008.
3. "Fast Facts about American Religion," Hartford Institute for Religion Research. http://hirr.hartsem.edu/research/fastfacts/fast_facts.html, accessed June 21, 2013.
4. Cited by Mary Fairchild in "Christianity Today—General Statistics and Facts of Christianity," About.com Christianity, http://christianity.about.com/od/denominations/p/christiantoday.htm, accessed June 21, 2013.
5. Dietrich Bonhoeffer, *The Cost of Discipleship* (New York: Touchstone, 1959), Foreword, 63, 64.
6. Ibid.
7. Church Society.org, www.churchsociety.org.
8. Keep God in America.com, http://www.keepgodinamerica.com/statistics.asp; www.religioustolerence.org.

9. Wade Clark Roof and Sr. Mary Johnson, "Baby Boomers and the Return to the Churches," http://hirr.hartsem.edu/bookshelf/Church&Denomgrowth/ch&dngrw-ch14.pdf, 293–94, accessed June 21, 2013.

10. Robert Lewis, *The Church of Irresistible Influence* (Grand Rapids: Zondervan, 2001), 31.

11. Gary Mortara, *Be a Man!* (San Leandro, CA: Iron Men of Faith, 2005), 77.

CHAPTER 2

1. J. Heinrich Arnold, *Discipleship* (United Kingdom: Plough Publishing House, 1994), Introduction.

2. "Nowhere to Go but Down: The Edge of Dying," *Deadliest Catch.* Originally aired June 5, 2012, on the Discovery Channel. A clip of the scene referred to can be seen at http://dsc.discovery.com/tv-shows/deadliest-catch/videos/season-8-episode-9-videos.htm.

3. Paul Meier, *Blue Genes* (Carol Stream, IL: Tyndale House Publishers, 2005), 112.

4. Patrick Morley, *Pastoring Men* (Chicago, IL: Moody Publishers, 2008), 47.

5. A.C. Myers, The *Eerdmans Bible Dictionary* (Grand Rapids: Wm B. Eerdmans Publishing Company, 1987), 631.

6. Jim Putman, et al. "Equipping Disciples Who Make Disciples," *Real-Life Discipleship Training Manual* (Colorado Springs, CO: NavPress, 2010), 29–38.

7. Bob Buford, *Halftime* (Grand Rapids: Zondervan, 1994), 18, 20.

CHAPTER 3

1. Christopher B. Adsit, *Personal Disciple-Making* (Nashville: Thomas Nelson, 1993), 35.

2. Pat Morley, *Pastoring Men: What Works, What Doesn't, and Why It Matters Now More than Ever* (Chicago, IL: Moody Publishers, 2009), 78.

3. We will further address the concept of "relational platforms" in a later chapter.

4. "Fast Facts about American Religion," Hartford Institute for Religion Research, http://hirr.hartsem.edu/research/fastfacts/fast_facts.html, accessed June 21, 2013.

5. "America's Families and Living Arrangements: 2012," U.S. Census Bureau, http://www.census.gov/hhes/families/data/cps2012.html, accessed June 21, 2013.

6. Jim Putman, Excerpts from *Discipleship Sermon Series*, Fall 2005.

CHAPTER 4

1. George Barna, *The Power of Vision* (Ventura, CA: Regal Books, 1992), 11.
2. U.S. Department of State, "Independent States in the World Fact Sheet," Bureau of Intelligence and Research, Washington, D.C., January 3, 2012, http://www.state.gov/s/inr/rls/4250.htm, accessed June 26, 2013.
3. Rick Warren, (speech sponsored by the National Coalition of Ministry to Men), Saddleback Church, Lake Forest, California. September 13, 2012.
4. Jim Putman, *Real-Life Discipleship* (Colorado Springs: NavPress, 2010), 62.
5. John Stott, *Between Two Worlds: The Challenge of Preaching Today* (Grand Rapids: Wm B. Eerdmans, 1982), 180.

CHAPTER 5

1. James M. Houston, *The Mentored Life* (Colorado Springs: NavPress, 2002), 17.
2. National Fish Habitat Partnership, ASA Releases New Fishing Statistics Report, "Sportfishing in America: An Economic Force for Conservation – 2013," http://fishhabitat.org/news/asa-releases-new-fishing-statistics-report, accessed June 27, 2013.
3. Statistic Brain, http://www.statisticbrain.com/hunting-statistics/2013, accessed June 27, 2013.
4. Rudyard Kipling, "If," http://www.poemhunter.com/poem/if/, accessed June 21, 2013.

CHAPTER 6

1. Great-Quotes.com, http://www.great-quotes.com/quote/145083, accessed June 21, 2013.
2. Theodore Roosevelt, *The Strenuous Life: Essays and Addresses* (New York: Charles Scribner's Sons, 1903), 4.

CHAPTER 7

1. Ken Carpenter, *Spirit of Revival* magazine, August 1982.
2. Joseph Henry Thayer, *Greek-English Lexicon of the New Testament* (New York: Harper Brothers, 1899), 389.
3. Edward E. Hindson, *Men of the Promise* (Eugene, OR: Harvest House Publishers, 1996), 17.

CHAPTER 8

1. Peter Marshall, speech at the University of Pittsburgh, 1946.
2. Ken Carpenter, *Spirit of Revival,* August 1982.
3. Larry Chouinard, *Matthew: The College Press NIV Commentary* (Joplin, MO: College Press, 1997), S. Mt 10:34.

CHAPTER 9

1. Dietrich Bonhoeffer, *The Cost of Discipleship* (New York: Touchstone, 1995), 57, 59.
2. William Bennett, *The Book of Man* (Nashville: Thomas Nelson, 2011), 20–21.
3. Ken Carpenter, *Spirit of Revival,* August 1982.
4. Jim Putman, *Real-Life Discipleship* (Colorado Springs: NavPress, 2010), 43–72.
5. Ibid., 49–51.
6. Ibid., 52–54.
7. Ibid., 55–58.

CHAPTER 10

1. The Counseling Team International, www.thecounselingteam.com/interactive/quotes/Education.pdf, accessed June 21, 2013.
2. *The Confessions of St. Augustine,* Bishop of Hippo, Book 1, Chapter 1.
3. Bill Hull, *Jesus Christ, Disciple Maker* (Grand Rapids: Baker, 2004), 85.

CHAPTER 11

1. Charles R. Swindoll, *Laugh Again* (Nashville: Thomas Nelson, 1992), 40.

CHAPTER 12

1. Sue Mallory, *The Equipping Church* (Grand Rapids: Zondervan, 2001), 37.
2. Info found at *Wikipedia*'s entry for "United States Navy SEALs," http://en.wikipedia.org/wiki/United_States_Navy_SEALs, accessed June 21, 2013.
3. Jeffrey Arnold, *The Big Book on Small Groups* (Downers Grove, IL: InterVarsity Press, 1992), ch. 2.
4. Ibid.
5. John Drescher, "A Parable of Fishless Fishermen," *The Discipleship Journal,* Vol. 18, p. 42. (Colorado Springs: Navpress)

BIBLIOGRAPHY

Aldrich, Joseph C. *Gentle Persuasion*. Portland, OR: Multnomah Press, 1988.

Arnold, J. Heinrich. *Discipleship*. Farmington, PA: Plough Publishing House, 2007.

———— *Life-Style Evangelism*. Portland, OR: Multnomah Press, 1981.

———— *Living Proof*. Colorado Springs: NavPress, 1989.

Bennett, William J. *The Book of Virtues*. New York: Simon and Schuster, 1993.

Bonhoeffer, Dietrich. *The Cost of Discipleship*. New York: Macmillan Publishing Co., 1963.

Boreham, F. W. *The Uttermost Star*. London: Epworth Press, 1935.

Coleman, Robert E. *The Master Plan of Evangelism*. Grand Rapids: Fleming H. Revell, 1993.

Downer, Phil, *Eternal Impact*. Eugene, OR.: Harvest House Publishers, 1997.

Hull, Bill. *Jesus Christ, Disciple Maker*. Grand Rapids: Fleming H. Revell, 1990.

Jones, E. Stanley. *How to Pray*. Nashville: Abingdon Press, 1979.

Logos Bible Software. *Logos*. Bellington,WA: Logos Bible Software.

MacDonald, Gordon. *Ordering Your Private World*. Nashville: Thomas Nelson Publishers, 1985.

———— *Restoring Your Spiritual Passion*. Nashville: Thomas Nelson Publishers, 1986.

Morley, Patrick. *Pastoring Men*. Chicago: Moody Publishers, 2009.

———— *No Man Left Behind*. Chicago: Moody Publishers, 2006.

Needham, David C. *Close to His Majesty*. Portland, OR: Multnomah Press, 1987.

Nun, Mendel. *The Sea of Galilee and Its Fishermen in the New Testament*. Ein Gev, Israel: Kibbutz Ein Gev Publishing, 1989.

Ogilvie, Lloyd J. *Making Stress Work for You*. Waco, TX: Word, 1984.

Petersen, Jim. *Lifestyle Discipleship*. Colorado Springs: NavPress, 1993.

———— *Living Proof*. Colorado Springs: NavPress, 1989.

Phillips, J. B. *Your God Is Too Small*. New York: Macmillan Publishing Co., 1961.

Putman, Jim *Real-Life Discipleship*. Colorado Springs: NavPress, 2010.

Jim Putman, Avery T. Willis Jr., Brandon Guindon, Bill Krause. *Real-Life Discipleship Training Manual.* Colorado Springs: NavPress, 2010.

Richards, Lawrence O. *The 365-Day Devotional Commentary.* Wheaton, IL: Victor Books, 1931.

Stecker, Chuck *Anchor Points Seminar Booklet.* Littleton, CO.: A Chosen Generation, 2007.

Swindoll, Charles R. *Discipleship—Bible Study Guide.* Fullerton, CA: Insight for Living, 1990.

——— *Laugh Again.* Waco, TX: Word, 1991.

Thayer, Joseph Henry. *Greek-English Lexicon of the New Testament.* New York: Harper Brothers Publishers, 1899.